Get to Grips
with
The Yips

www.scaryputter.com

First printing 2020
Copyright © WHP Jackson 2020
ISBN 9798683744892

Front cover photograph © Jason Livy : Woking Golf Club. 16th hole.

All royalties for this book will be donated to the Olivia Hodson Cancer Fund, a special purpose fund within Great Ormond Street Hospital Charity.

Get to Grips with The Yips

How to Fix Your Putting and Love Golf Again

Peter Jackson

If you can keep your head when all about you
Are losing theirs and blaming it on you,
If you can trust yourself when all men doubt you,
But make allowance for their doubting too;
If you can wait and not be tired by waiting,
Or being lied about, don't deal in lies,
Or being hated, don't give way to hating,
And yet don't look too good, nor talk too wise:

If you can dream—and not make dreams your master;
If you can think—and not make thoughts your aim;
If you can meet with Triumph and Disaster
And treat those two impostors just the same;
If you can bear to hear the truth you've spoken
Twisted by knaves to make a trap for fools,
Or watch the things you gave your life to, broken,
And stoop and build 'em up with worn-out tools:

If you can make one heap of all your winnings
And risk it on one turn of pitch-and-toss,
And lose, and start again at your beginnings
And never breathe a word about your loss;
If you can force your heart and nerve and sinew
To serve your turn long after they are gone,
And so hold on when there is nothing in you
Except the Will which says to them: 'Hold on!'

If you can talk with crowds and keep your virtue,
Or walk with Kings—nor lose the common touch,
If neither foes nor loving friends can hurt you,
If all men count with you, but none too much;
If you can fill the unforgiving minute
With sixty seconds' worth of distance run,
Yours is the Earth and everything that's in it,
And—which is more—you'll be a Man, my son!

If......by Rudyard Kipling (1943)

CONTENTS

FOREWORD

Everybody has heroes.

They provide a point of focus, particularly if you are young and have not yet worked out who you are. They represent an ideal towards which you can strive, even if that ideal ultimately turns out to be less than perfect. Hero worship typically starts with your parents (heroes forever in my eyes), or perhaps a cartoon character. However, at some point – usually around puberty – allegiance can switch, often to a rock star, a sporting god, or heaven forbid, a social-media influencer. Rarely to a scientist. You need to pick your heroes carefully, of course. People seldom do. It's not the way it works. It's almost like you don't have a choice.

My Dad was a keen golfer. Not only have I inherited the disease, but his influence seems to have extended to my choice of heroes. In my case, they were all golfers (except for Albert Einstein. I liked science too) – in chronological order Jack Nicklaus, Tom Watson, Seve Ballesteros and Bernhard Langer. I trust you have heard of them. By the way, I am reasonably sure puberty wasn't involved for me. I always loved golf. Seve was undoubtedly my superhero, Tom a close second, and Jack a solid third. It took a long time for Bernhard to creep up the rankings.

Bernhard possessed a rather mechanical swing without the brisk rhythm of Watson or the majesty of Seve in full flow. The wins in his early career were less frequent and less exciting. His record will never stand up to big Jack's. It is almost unfair to compare him with Seve. Everybody seemed like an actuary compared to the Spanish conquistador. Whilst Seve swash-buckled his way with a carefree spirit of adventure, Bernhard plotted his route around the course, studiously verifying yardages to the nearest millimetre and carrying himself like a robotic, teutonic prince. He did once climb up a tree to play a shot in a tournament, and I really enjoyed that, but the decision to do so might merely have been the output of the computer in his head. Perhaps he is a cyborg; part-man, part-machine; a bit like Arnold Schwarzenegger in Terminator, only much more ruthless and a little less expressive. He certainly did not show much emotion on the golf course. Perhaps ice flows through his veins.

That is enough character assassination for now. Obviously, I loved Seve and Tom and Jack. The reason Bernhard made the cut into my personal Hall of Fame is that he faced and overcame the greatest challenge in golf: the yips. Yes, we are daring to mention them by name. Nothing bad will happen. They are not Voldemort.

Back in 1988 – in the days when world-class golfers played much of their golf in the UK – I had the good fortune to spectate at the European Open at Sunningdale. I spotted Bernhard on the course and decided to follow and learn from the master. He was 1 under par for the 6 holes I was with him, which was good but not impressive for such a top player. What is perhaps more significant is that on each of the greens he missed a putt of less than six feet, three of them no more than a yard. Whilst every approach shot was rifled surgically at the pin, none of the putts looked remotely close to dropping, but since one of them was for eagle he finally made a 2-putt birdie. It was not easy to watch, as I was already uncomfortably familiar with the yips myself.

However, as most of us know, Bernhard is nothing if not a hard worker. He recovered from what looked like a terminal case and went on to win countless tournaments. Furthermore, every time the demons reappeared, he recreated his stroke and rose phoenix-like from the ashes to even greater heights. Go to the PGA tour website and view his record. It is astonishing. To have such a career and remain a world-class putter despite those demons is without equal in the world of golf.

Tom Watson has faced his own putting challenges too. Surely the greatest links golfer of all time and perhaps an even greater gentleman, his troubles were less than Bernhard's, but were perhaps less comprehensively resolved. As for the deity that is the Golden Bear, the yips would never have dared to go anywhere near him. Seve had the odd issue with his driver but his putting remained an incomparable thing of beauty. Tragically, his was a far greater battle to fight. Like many of his fans around the world, I never met him, but I still miss him.

That clearly leaves Bernhard – a perennial winner on the senior circuit – as the person who should be writing this book, but as far as I know he has kept relatively quiet about his demons. Maybe he is just lazy after all, or perhaps he is too busy slaying humans on the Champion's Tour.

Whatever the reason, thank you Bernhard. This book is inspired by you.

But it is dedicated to my Dad.

LAYING DOWN THE GROUND RULES

GOLF IS THE WINDOW TO THE SOUL

I love golf. It is a wonderful game in so many ways; endlessly challenging, infinitely variable, utterly infuriating. It gets under your skin, in the process providing lifelong friendships and revealing you for the person you are, whether you like it or not. No other game I know can challenge it for complexity or difficulty (although to be fair I have always thought snooker was impossible).

This book has a laser focus: to describe, define and reduce nervousness in golfers, particularly (but not exclusively) those suffering its most extreme form, the yips. I thought about giving them a capital Y but that is a form of respect they do not deserve. They will forever be lower case.

Science Corner

I also love science. One of the ambitions of this book is to show that scientific methods can be used to inform and confirm how to play the game. I will be attempting to create an objective system for decision-making in this most subjective of sports, offering logical answers to emotional questions.

Most golf books are short on scientific content, but there a few around. My favourites are "Dave Pelz's Putting Bible" by Dave Pelz (who was a genuine NASA scientist), "Every Shot Counts" by Mark Broadie (who is a professor at Columbia Business School), and all the books of Bob Rotella, the leading psychologist in the game.

From time to time, you will come across the **Science Corner**, in which I offer an optional, scientific way of looking at things. I will loosely include mathematics under the science umbrella (some people think maths is an art not a science), but be assured, we are only going to do adding, subtracting, multiplying, and dividing. We golfers can sometimes get stuck in a rut, repeatedly attempting the same thing, and going nowhere. The better offerings from the Science Corner are designed to offer an alternative to your gut instincts, and provide a hitherto unthought of path out of that rut. You will also find an occasional reference to my website, www.scaryputter.com , where you can download an Excel spreadsheet and do some of the analysis yourself.

Pseudo-Science Alert: During our Science Corner moments, I will occasionally produce a formula and table of results, often based on data about my own game. *Never take these tables as universal truth*. They are an illustration of *my* game, not yours, and they are not precise. The aim is for you to adopt the technique and apply it to yourself.

PUTTING PROBLEMS

Despite my love of golf, there have been times when I have considered giving it up. Thankfully, that never happened, but the disillusionment was so great that it was a close call at times. The cause of this anguish was of course putting, the "game within the game". Not just bad putting, but uncontrollable, spasmodic putting that destroyed my confidence, my self-esteem and any of the joy that golf can and should provide.

This is *not* a book about me. I'm not an interesting subject, even to myself. I prefer not to be the loudest voice in the room. I will try hard to keep a lid on it.

This is a book about you and how to enjoy golf and your life more.

That may sound pompous, but that really is its agenda, hidden amongst the flippant half-jokes and the technical stuff.

The true purpose of this book is to offer hope to others who have travelled the same road as me, are currently exasperated with their game and might otherwise hang up their clubs. Golf is too great a pastime to let that happen. Golf is also medically proven to extend your life, so if I can help a few people to stay on the course, then I can claim to be saving lives and contributing to society.

DO NOT DISMISS THIS BOOK JUST BECAUSE YOU DO NOT HAVE THE YIPS

The most extreme form of putting problem is the yips, and we will deal with them in this book. However, they are just part of a continuum of anxieties you may encounter whilst playing golf. They are also not contagious. This book can help you *irrespective* of whether you have the yips. Most importantly, it will provide a framework to ensure that they never visit you in the future. Where putting issues are concerned, prevention is many times better than cure.

"ONCE YOU GET THEM, YOU'VE GOT THEM"

Many people believe that once you get the yips, you will never be able to rid yourself of them. *This is patently untrue*. The yips are both a neurological problem and a psychological problem. This book will show you how to fix both elements, or at the very least how to circumvent the yips and remain a functional golfer.

WRITING STYLE

When I first told my son I was writing a book, he asked me what literary style I was going to use. That floored me somewhat. I didn't know literature had *styles*. I am more of a numbers guy. My initial reaction was that my desired style would be "pithy one-liners with a few equations", something that could have been a co-creation by David Feherty and Dave Pelz. However, the Pulitzer Prize jury don't recognise that as a genre just yet, and I fear I may have got it the wrong way round and ended up with Dave Pelz's humour and David Feherty's scientific insight.

After careful consideration I decided that my chosen style will be "conversational". This book will be a conversation between me – the worldly-wise Professor Dumbledore – and you – his brilliant, adoring pupil Harry Potter. Admittedly, I do more of the talking, but you get to play Harry Potter. If you prefer Star Wars, then you can be Luke Skywalker instead. Happy to be Yoda I am. Let's complete the set. I will be Gandalf and you can choose between Bilbo and Frodo.

By the way, I am probably the last person in the world to have realised this, but have you noticed that The Lord of the Rings, Star Wars, Harry Potter, and Game of Thrones are all essentially the same story? The triumph of Good over Evil with a bit of hocus pocus thrown in. Apologies if you have never read or watched them, as I may have just given away the ending. The only plus is that now you don't need to. That will save you a great deal of time, and you can devote it to golf instead.

Stay the course with this book and not only will you live a yip-free life, but you will also be a record breaker. In real life, I'm not exactly renowned as a conversationalist. Let's just say that in person my one-liners are less frequent. However, they do remain equally unfunny. Finish this book and you will have taken part in the longest conversation I have ever had.

So, it's decided. This book is about both you and me, comrades joining our powers to banish the evil Lord Voldemort to Azkaban.

One last thing on the style of the book. If you come across a few oddities in terms of spelling, punctuation, meaning or logic, please don't worry. It's probably because you are American and I am English. Two countries divided by a single language.

IRONY

It might be worthwhile to clarify that when I suggested in the foreword that Bernhard Langer was lazy, I didn't really mean it. I was being ironic. I do it too much, and I fear it is as close to humour as you will find in this book. Unless I'm being sarcastic. Just be on the lookout. In the same vein, I'm also reasonably sure Bernhard isn't a cyborg.

AN EARLY APOLOGY

No, not to Bernhard. That will come later when I am compelled to do so in court. You have already seen me compare my battle with the yips to one between fictional powers of good and evil. When I run out of fantasy-hero metaphors, I tend to fall into the lazy trap of comparing the yips to life-threatening diseases. As I write, we are in the midst of a global pandemic. Problems with golf are as nothing in comparison and I can only apologise if anything offends you.

COLOURS

I'll be using colour-coding throughout:

Green is Good

Yellow is OK

Orange is Dangerous

Red is Bad

WOMEN GOLFERS

I regret and apologise that all of the examples used in this book are male golfers (although two of my favourite long-game swings are those of Annika Sorenstam and Stacey Lewis). I have been less than inclusive to the many excellent lady golfers out there. Be assured, the yips are gender blind and the advice in this book will apply equally to you.

LEFTIES

If you are left-handed, you are already quite used to stupid right-handers forgetting you exist. Everything I say and show will be assuming you are right-handed and that lefties are capable of reversing polarity for themselves.

INSTRUCTION: HIT OR MISS?

My experience of teachers and teaching is not universally positive. Whether academic or golf-related, I have found that whilst some people and some ideas help me, others just don't. There are several potential reasons for this (my own stubbornness being the bookmaker's favourite), but just bear it in mind. There are many suggestions in this book, almost all of which I have attempted myself, most (but not all) of which I find useful. They won't all work for you, and you should expect to disagree with me occasionally, if not frequently. Let's make a deal: I will promise not to take it personally when you fail to agree with me, as long as you promise to keep your eyes on the prize and stay on track. It is OK to lose a few battles along the way as long as you win the war.

NO CHEATING OR PEEKING

Golfers never cheat, do they? I wouldn't dare accuse you of that. However, it is very tempting with a book like this to open it up somewhere in the middle and randomly start reading. I would advise against that, as each chapter is designed to build on what precedes it. A few of them may make no sense unless you've read up to that point. We are trying to construct a building capable of withstanding a hurricane. If you haven't built the foundations and walls properly, there's no way the roof is going to stay on.

OBJECTIVES

Let me be crystal clear. **This book is not going to make you a world-class putter.**

The aim is to make you a better putter, more confident, and more able to enjoy the game I love. If you are really struggling with your game, my hope would be to make you an average putter.

If you are already a decent putter, but are occasionally nervous, then this book will help you to improve. More importantly though, it will prevent the slow decline in confidence that can happen to so many over time.

When you reach the end of this book and I am happy you are in a good place, I will release you into the care of the real experts who can teach you about all the other elements of putting. I could not be happier if you then became a world-class putter with their help.

WHAT KIND OF GOLFER ARE YOU?

Before we go any further, I need to do some calibration. Here are a few questions to help you identify what kind of golfer you are.

I'm going to start gently:
- Have you ever felt nervous when you putt?
- Does it get worse on the 18th hole of a competition?
- Do you dislike 3 footers?
- Have you ever taken more than 40 putts a round?
- Do you own more than 5 putters?
- Is the putter your least favourite club?
- Have you ever believed you were born a bad putter?
- Have you ever thought it unfair that putting was a part of golf?
- Have you ever completely frozen over a putt?
- Have you ever felt your putter was a separate life form?
- Have you ever putted a ball completely off a flat green?
- Have you ever double-hit a putt?
- Have you ever intentionally lagged a flat 2-foot putt?
- Does putting sometimes feel like you're being tasered?
- Has putting made you want to give up golf?

That's probably enough; any more questions and one of us might start crying.

Let's try to get some structure round this. My questions are intentionally listed in order of severity. Some people may only answer yes to the first couple. Others, like me, may have completed the whole set at some point in their lives.

GOLFING HIERARCHY

Nervousness in golf is normal. Pressure is an everyday part of the game and to whatever extent we can, we need to enjoy it, relish it even. We will look at that in detail much later, but for the purposes of illustration I am going to divide the world's golfers into four categories in relation to their putting.

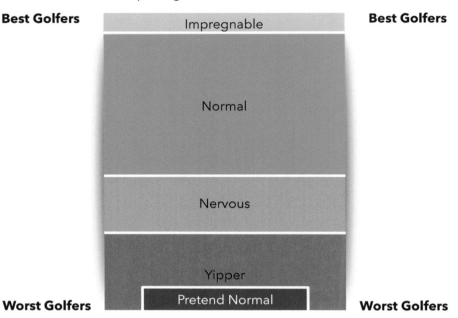

IMPREGNABLE GOLFERS

I can only think of three members of this category: Bobby Jones (he called his Grand Slam the Impregnable Quadrilateral), Jack Nicklaus and Tiger Woods (I know Tiger's putting stats aren't quite so good nowadays but his status is safe).

NORMAL GOLFERS

The vast majority of the world's golfers are in this category. At the top end we have tour pros and elite amateurs. It can go right down to 36 handicappers and even complete beginners. Their "normality" comes from them viewing putting as just part of the greater game.

They feel pressure when faced with short putts, bunkers, bare chipping lies, out of bounds fences. It can get worse if they are on the 18th in a game that matters to them. We are human beings. That is how we are wired.

Normal golfers will probably tick a few of the boxes above, but not many. Some are better at dealing with the pressure than others, but that is true in many parts of life.

Some Normal golfers are terrible putters, but that does *not* necessarily make them yippers. They are probably just bad at everything else in putting. They may be new to the game, have poor judgement, or maybe nobody ever told them how to read a green.

Occasionally, a Normal golfer will drift into the next category.

NERVOUS GOLFERS

We all know a few Nervous golfers. They worry about things a bit too much. They let things get into their head. They sometimes react poorly under pressure. They might lift their head too soon, too often. If you were playing them in the scratch knockout, you might consider not giving them a 2-footer.

Nervous golfers may answer yes to a few more of my questions, but they are not yippers. They may well take more putts than the Normal guys, but not significantly so. Some Nervous golfers even think they might be a yipper. They are not, but unless they are careful, they may be going in that direction.

YIPPERS

There is some debate as to how many yippers there are out there. In one piece of research, it was found that between 32% and 48% of single-figure handicappers admitted to yip-like symptoms. However, it was a questionnaire, and we know from elections that you can't necessarily trust what people say in questionnaires, particularly when only 39% of people actually responded to it. I think 20% is a much more likely percentage for yippers, with perhaps half of those suffering extreme symptoms. Yippers have essentially lost control of the putter at impact. I would characterise the double hit as a final stage yip phenomenon. Outcomes are typically extremely poor, often involving a sand wedge for the next shot. Not all yippers are quite so bad, but they all have real difficulty in controlling impact. Some like to pretend they are not yippers at all....

PRETEND NORMAL

These guys are a subset of the yippers, so they do not merit a separate category. **They are in denial**. They have the yips but are hoping nobody will notice. They refuse to acknowledge their problem, and consequently do nothing to fix it. They are too proud to try anything that might single them out as weak. Mr Pretend Normal is the worst kind of yipper because he will never recover. Like alcoholism, the yips first require you to acknowledge you have a problem. Only then can you go and fix it. Perversely, Pretend Normal golfers are the least likely people to read a book like this, even though they are the most in need. If you know one of them, and you think this book is useful, please recommend it to him or her.

WHICH TYPE OF PUTTER ARE YOU?

You may have recognised yourself already in one of these categories. However, not only is it probably far from clear right now, but golfers are constantly moving within and between these categories. That is the entire point of the book.

As I will explain later, my life history as a putter goes along the following lines:

Age	Type of Putter
7 to 13	Normal
14 to 18	Nervous
19 to 44	Yipper (pretending to be Normal)
45 onwards	Nervous (working hard to be Normal)

I will never enter the Impregnable category. It is full. Bobby Jones has moved out, but Jack and Tiger are not accepting applications.

TRANSITION BETWEEN TYPES OF PUTTERS

Let's look again at the hierarchy:

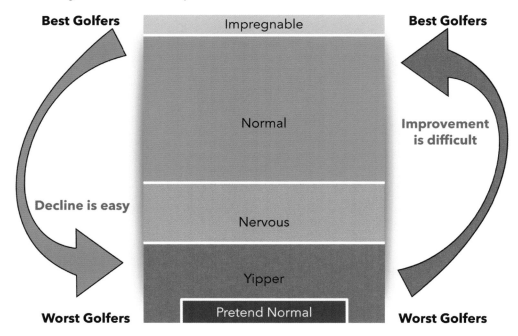

Over a period of time (usually years), a Normal golfer can develop scar tissue from a series of disappointing moments and find himself in the Nervous camp. Pile on a few more bad experiences and he might tip over the edge and become a Yipper.

This process of decline from Normal to Nervous is usually gradual, or what mathematicians might call a "continuous function".

It is still the same gradual process as you drift downwards within the ranks of the Nervous.

There can come a point though, if you are unlucky or unwary, at which you fall off a cliff and become a yipper. That fall down the cliff face is what a mathematician would call a "discontinuous function".

Once you have arrived in the land of yip, it is tricky to get back. You cannot just click your heels 3 times like Dorothy in the Wizard of Oz and say, "There's no place like home".

You also cannot go all the way back in one large step. There is no way to transition directly from a yipper to a Normal golfer. Your train to destination Normal must stop at station Nervous on the way.

PUTTING IS LIKE SWIMMING UP THE ZAMBEZI

Fighting nerves in putting is similar to swimming upstream in a river. Your goal is a positive, relaxed frame of mind, and it is upstream. The current is always fighting you, dragging you away from your target. Things are not too bad when you are a Normal golfer. Just keep paddling and you will stay where you are. The same is almost true for a Nervous golfer. You're further downstream. The current is a little stronger and you must work harder. However, if you let things slip, you will start to hear some noise and see plumes of spray around you. Beware. You are in the Zambezi and Victoria Falls is getting close.

Transitioning from a Nervous golfer to a yipper is like going over a waterfall; an unpleasant drop followed by a great deal of shock. What is worse is that once you are down below the falls, no matter how hard you try, you are not getting back up without a different mode of transport.

WHAT PART OF THE ZAMBEZI ARE YOU SWIMMING IN?

Impregnable Golfers
Jack and Tiger

Normal Golfers

Nervous Golfers

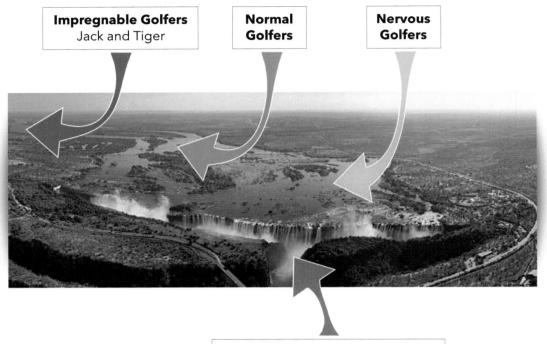

Yippers
I was here from 1984 to 2009
Pretend Normal golfers never leave

Science Corner: The Yip Transition Matrix

This is the first Science Corner, and least useful. It is really just a warm-up. You can happily skip over it, but later on they are better and more valuable. Wherever possible I will add a visual or verbal alternative. In this case, I already have. It's the Zambezi.

Here is how I would express the whole process to a mathematician. It describes how things can transform from one state to another.

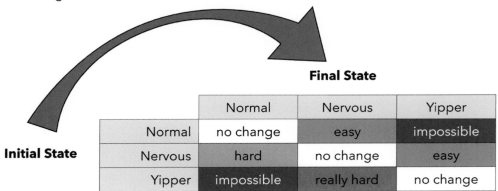

	Final State		
	Normal	Nervous	Yipper
Normal	no change	easy	impossible
Nervous	hard	no change	easy
Yipper	impossible	really hard	no change

The White boxes represent staying where you are (e.g. from Normal to Normal)

The Purple boxes remind us you cannot jump all the way (in either direction) from Normal putter to Yipper.

The Green boxes show how easy is it is to slip from Normal to Nervous golfer, and thence to being a Yipper.

The red box is the swimmer at the bottom of Victoria Falls, scratching his head and wondering how on earth he is going to get back up. It is really hard, but importantly **it is not impossible**.

The Orange box is telling us it is hard to transition from a Nervous putter to a Normal putter. The swimmer is just above Victoria Falls, and must watch out for crocs and keep swimming.

Pseudo-Science Alert: **Not great, was it?** I far prefer the Zambezi analogy and it is a good reminder for me that science is not always the answer.

Thankfully, I spared you any of the equations that a mathematician would have wanted to put in the boxes, and the maths lesson is now over.

WHAT TYPE OF GOLFER ARE YOU?

Like the proverbial bus, just when we've introduced one colour coding system, another one turns up.

Red Light: Stop

If you are an *Impregnable* golfer, you have a clean bill of health and need read no further. You are also either Jack Nicklaus or Tiger Woods. Hello, I am a big fan.

Amber Light: Proceed With Caution

If you are a *Normal* or *Nervous* golfer, then you should carry on. You may not have the yips , but you need to make sure you never succumb to them in the future. As I mentioned at the very outset, the yips are not contagious, and you are quite safe. I will only focus on positive things.

If you are swimming happily at the top end of the Normal scale and have better things to do, I understand. However, you may know someone less fortunate than yourself who might benefit from this book, in which case please give it immediately to the most deserving candidate. Even better, throw away your copy and just recommend it instead. That way I might get book sales up a bit.

Green Light: Go

If you are a yipper, then this is the book for you. You are not alone.

3

GOLF BOOKS

WHO SHOULD WRITE THIS BOOK?
Bernhard, obviously.

It's unlikely you have heard of me before, unless you were thinking perhaps of the director of the Lord of the Rings. He shares my name, but our obsessions are quite different.

Before I bore you with my qualifications, it may be better to focus on who is *not* qualified to talk about the yips. Use the correct process and you may discover to your surprise that my experience is just what you need.

PUTTING BOOKS
There are many putting books available, and I have read most of them. The majority are written by experienced, well regarded tournament professionals or lifelong golf coaches. Most of them are excellent; logically organised into relevant chapters and intended to turn a mediocre putter into a better one.

You should read them, but it's important to think about the order you read them in.

If you are having nervous problems with your putting, the issue with almost all of these books is that **they are completely focused on the wrong thing**.

Let's take the most extreme example. What is the point of considering the effect of grain on a 10-foot putt if you are just hoping to get down in 2 without totally embarrassing yourself? A few of these excellent books even have a chapter on the yips, but they often seem to be there as a reluctant afterthought.

Address your nerve issues first, then read the putting books afterwards.

Have you ever received well-meaning advice from your (non-yipping) playing partners about keeping your head still, or quietening the hands, or just using the big muscles, or rocking the shoulders? How helpful did you find it? Not very, because they simply don't understand what you are experiencing. They have literally no clue.

The only person qualified to give advice on putting nerves is someone who has
>   **a) had the yips,** and
>   **b) beaten the yips.**

Being a world class putter is not a qualification to advise on the yips. In many ways it is an *impediment*.

That rules out Dave Stockton, or Jack Nicklaus, or Brad Faxon, or Ken Brown, or pretty much any of the true greats. In my opinion, it also rules out several excellent golf coaches who have been fortunate enough to escape the yips themselves.

BOOKS AND RESEARCH ABOUT YIPPING

Hank Haney has already written this book. He wrote "Fix the Yips Forever", which is crystal clear about its intentions. You should read this book. I did so when it came out (in 2006), and I think I am fixed, but *forever* is a strong word. For me, the road to recovery came partly through Hank's help, partly through that of others, and partly from my own experimentation (which he recommends), including to some degree the appliance of science. Hank is a world-class teacher and has all the qualifications. He suffered from the yips for decades, although in his case they were primarily with the driver. His book covers forms of yipping throughout golf: putting, chipping and even the long game. I hope that my book will add something to what he laid down in the putting section, in some small way like Sir Isaac Newton when he said he was "standing on the shoulders of giants" (i.e. learning from and building on the work of his illustrious forbears).

Hank worked closely with **Dr Christian Marquardt**, the German neuroscientist who invented SAM PuttLab. I don't think Christian has written a book as such; he is a serious scientist and writes proper scientific research, frequently with the Mayo Clinic. Amongst many other things he advises the German national golf team on putting.

Bob Rotella is a world authority about yips and the psychology of the game. He discusses them in many of his books. We will be taking advice from him later.

Dave Pelz is my favourite golf coach. He is the Neil Armstrong of golf coaches. His book "Dave Pelz's Putting Bible" is indeed what it says on the tin. 400 pages of densely packed scientific wisdom. Only 4 of the pages deal with the yips, but they are excellent pages. Buy this book.

Another serious attempt to help with the yips is hidden away in "The Lost Art of Putting" by **Karl Morris** and **Gary Nicol**. It has 7 pages of material in its chapter on the yips, specifically referencing the highly respected **Dr Debbie Crews**, whose work I like very much. But again, it is only 7 pages out of 140.

David McKenzie has written "How to Cure the yips". David is a successful golf psychologist and focuses on the mental side of the game.

Patrick J. Cohn is a sports psychologist who has various drills, videos and articles on his website putting yips.com

Donn Levine wrote "Outwit the yips", the story of his own challenges and solutions. His experience and recommendations are similar to some you will find in this book, although the approach is quite different.

The most accessible scientific article on the yips I have come across is **"The Science of the Yips"**, written by Robert E. Wharen, Debbie J. Crews, and Charles H. Adler. You can find it in the Routledge International Handbook of Golf Science, which in addition to that article contains 38 other pieces of academic golf research. It's not for everyone (it's at the outer edge of even my scientific tolerances), but I will try to summarise it later.

Science Corner

Try googling for golf books about yipping. **There are very few out there.** I have listed some above. Beyond that, there is very little.

Interestingly, the tag line on Hank's book is "The First and Only Guide You Need to Solve the Game's Worst Curse". At least now you have a little more choice.

The following is a scientific way of demonstrating why there are so few:

We are going to use a process of *elimination*.

The most famous calculation of this type is the Drake equation, which astronomers use to estimate the number of places in the Universe where civilisation exists (between 4 and 211 according to one study, with the most likely number being 36). Sometimes I wonder if civilisation occurs *anywhere* in the universe, including earth, but that will be another book.

Our starting point for the calculation is a little easier than that for Drake, in which you begin by estimating how many stars there are in the universe. Not easy. In our case, we know roughly how many people inhabit our planet, so we'll start with them.

Criteria for Elimination	Explanation	Remaining Candidates
The world's Population	A good place to start	8 billion
You are not a golfer	Sensible	50 million
You are not an excellent golfer	We want to learn from the best. Less than 2% of golfers are scratch or better	1 million
You have not had the full-blown yips	If you haven't had them, you cannot talk about them with any authority.	100,000
You have not recovered from the yips	You can't cure me of a disease you still have yourself. You're out	10,000
You don't have the experience	You must be a real addict to know enough to write a book on golf	1,000
You don't have the ability to explain it	Not everyone can teach. It is an undervalued skill	100
You don't have the desire or time	Bernhard can't be bothered. Clearly, others too	10

Here is perhaps a clearer way of expressing the same process:

The World	8 billion
Golfers	50 million
Excellent Golfers	1 million
Excellent golfers *with yips*	100,000
Excellent golfers *cured* of the yips	10,000
Excellent ex-yip golf *addicts*	1,000
Excellent ex-yip golf addicts who *can write*	100
Excellent ex-yip golf addicts who can and *want to* write	10

So, a scientist will tell you that there are about 10 people in the world both *qualified* and *likely* to write this book.

Maybe more, maybe less. There is plenty of uncertainty in each of the steps. The scientist would probably give you a range of possible numbers. Let's say 3 to 50.

But in case you haven't realised it yet, **I am still in the running**. I need to prove it to you, but I pass all the tests.

Isn't it amazing what science can do?

It is said that you should only write a book on a subject about which you have real knowledge. You may have spotted some sleight of hand in the analysis, but I hope by the end of the book you will agree I am able to write this one. The only way it would fit me more perfectly is if it also required encyclopaedic knowledge of the 0-60 times of 1980s hatchbacks, and the ability to play Beethoven's Moonlight sonata badly.

CHAPTER

THE FALL AND RISE OF A GOLF ADDICT

Perhaps that would have been a better title for the book. Too late now.

The next section may seem self-indulgent, but if you are seriously considering following my advice, you should probably check out my credentials carefully. Unlike Hank Haney or Dave Pelz, my reputation does not go before me, so I will need to work hard to convince you. It's also an excuse for me to sneak in some autobiographical stuff. You can skip it and move on to the pictures if you like. They are the proof, such as it is.

At the very least I assure you I will try to remain relevant. All my hilarious anecdotes will remain untold. I might put a few in the 10th reprint of the book.

Part 1 Jacko: The Early Years

OPEN VENUE

I grew up in Lytham, Lancashire, England, and from the age of 7 was lucky enough to play my golf at Royal Lytham & St Anne's, where Seve Ballesteros won The Open Championship twice and my Dad was a member. I never had a lesson but was a keen student of the game, endlessly studying my copy of Golf My Way by Jack Nicklaus; an excellent, benchmark golf book which to this day I recommend, even if somehow Jack omitted to include any mention of yips in the putting section.

HOME-SCHOOLED

I practiced at home a great deal. Outside, I would hit plastic airflow balls in the garden, desperately trying to avoid taking divots (and the associated parental displeasure), thereby developing a shallow, scooping action that has taken decades to correct. Indoors, I combined my Ben Hogan Equalizer wedge and a table tennis ball to practice chipping. To be fair, it was more about generating spin. Once you have backed up a 12-foot chip shot with a ping-pong ball on carpet you simply cannot get enough.

PUTTING ADDICT

We had an indoor practice hole for putting – a metal one with flaps on hinges that flipped up as the ball rolled in – and I putted a lot. I really mean a great deal. When I look back at how single-minded, silent and focussed I was then, it's quite amazing to see what a witty, popular raconteur I have become (this is my irony kicking in, just in case you believed the second part of that sentence). It's almost like I'm a super-unsuccessful version of Nick Faldo, who didn't make my top 4 golfers, but did make the subs bench.

I created an entire world tour of putting circuits around the house, but my standard putting practice was a 20-footer in the hallway. It had a 4-inch break from the left. The accepted wisdom on many links courses is that every putt breaks towards the sea. In our house every putt broke away from the stairs.

EARLY PROMISE

At that early age I was an excellent putter. My record was 27 putts in a row from 20 feet, which is OK for a 12-year-old. In case you are rightly a little suspicious, this wasn't one of those carpets that is so worn in the middle that it is effectively a self-correcting valley, like a bowling alley with bumpers. We were not particularly well-off, but the carpets were reasonable. About 11 on the stimp, too. Perfect. I was using a fake Ping putter my dad bought from a toy shop. I was using my long game grip, whatever that was. I wasn't thinking about stance or path or grip or face angle. I was like any other kid, just trying to knock the next one in. It all seemed so easy.

TEENAGE DISAPPOINTMENT

I was by no means a child prodigy, but by the time I was 13 I had a handicap of 10 (I think Seve was down to scratch at the same stage). Around this time, the thought struck me that even though I loved putting, longer putts were preferable to shorter ones. Once you were inside 8 feet you really were supposed to hole any putt, and there was little or no excuse if you didn't. My thoughts began to veer towards "don't miss" rather than "hole". In retrospect, that may have been a mistake.

I began to not fancy 3 footers. There is a form of self-delusional golf in which you give yourself any putt you don't fancy (in certain circles this is technically known as a "deem"), but in the real world you have to get it in the hole and I was beginning to struggle.

What followed was a slow but lengthy decline. Whilst my long game improved (despite the scoopy swing and a lack of tuition), my putting deteriorated.

Aged 16, my handicap was 5, a decent ball striker and a weak putter.

ACADEMIC AND SPORTING MEDIOCRITY

I liked mathematics and went to Oxford University to study it. In the first week it became abundantly clear to both me and my tutor that I was not a mathematician, so I spent most of my time playing golf. Plenty of guys on the PGA tour passed their college years in similar fashion, but my experience was a little different to theirs. I didn't play a strokeplay event in 3 years. It was all matchplay. I didn't have any coaching. I didn't go to the gym. Some alcohol was involved, usually paid for by the generous hosts at the excellent courses we were privileged to play.

At the end of those 3 years I emerged with a surprisingly acceptable degree and a stable handicap of 5. Under the surface, however, things had changed. I was a far better ball striker and a much worse putter. By this point I had already perfected the double hit.

Part 2 Jacko: The Lost Decades

From the late Eighties until 2009 I did all the things normal people do. Despite a tendency to laziness, I worked hard. I was in an intensive, all-or-nothing job for 20 years so had relatively little choice about the matter. I married a beautiful, tolerant wife and had 3 beautiful children. I was still playing golf once a fortnight, but never practiced. I still hadn't had a lesson. I was still failing to control my putter. The horrors shall remain untold; no need to frighten anybody. The only good thing was it happened infrequently because I wasn't playing much.

Part 3 Jacko: The Glory Years

At the age of 45, I left my job (you've probably guessed by now that I wasn't a stand-up comedian; I had been working for a bank) and took some time off. My golf handicap was still resolutely stuck at 5, so I decided to try a little harder now that I had both the time and opportunity.

I had my first ever golf lesson (thank you Hugh Marr) and discovered that on video my Adam Scott-like swing more closely resembled that of his grandmother. I worked hard on all aspects of my game, but putting was still an "issue". Things slowly improved. Here are the edited highlights. Please bear in mind I was 45 years old at the start of them.

Year	Handicap	Highlight
2010	5	Leaving the world of banking
2011	4	Nothing worth mentioning
2012	3	Won a couple of midweek Stablefords
2013	1	Became a WAGR ranked player by winning the 36-hole qualifying for the Surrey County Amateur. Everyone was surprised, not least me. I was thrashed in the matchplay stage.
2014	Scratch	Won a couple of club championships
2015	+1	Reached final qualifying for the European Senior Tour (yes, the professional one). Was cut on the final day around 8 shots away from getting a card.
2016	+1	Qualified as second reserve for the Senior Open Championship at Carnoustie. None of the old guys withdrew, so I never played in the actual tournament. Probably just as well.
2017	+1	Reached Final Qualifying (at Deal) for the Open Championship. Yes, The Open Championship. I missed out by a lot of shots but beat South African tour pro Zander Lombard. He will never live it down. I also missed out on playing in the Senior Open in a playoff (again) and reached the final of the President's Putter at Rye
2018	+1	Came 6th in the European Senior (over 50) Amateur Championship
2019	+1	This was the year I was going to win big. It did not happen. I was just very unlucky 38 times in a row
2020	+1	Covid-19 happened. So did lockdown. No competitions.

I like to tell myself I am still in the Glory Years. 2021 will be The Big One when I turn 55 and emerge to dominate the senior amateur circuit. My back tells me otherwise. Time will tell. For all I know, I may already have entered the next stage – **Jacko: The Twilight Years**.

What a story! Sony Pictures and Paramount are currently fighting over the film rights. I'm planning to get Rickie Fowler to play me.

OK. I believe you *had* the yips. But did you *beat* the yips?

Whilst I managed to win almost nothing over an entire decade, I hope you would agree that there was an improvement, particularly as time was not working in my favour.

If we are going to learn much from it, we need to look at that improvement objectively. Was it significant and where was the improvement?

DATA IS TRUTH
My handicap improved by 6 shots between the ages of 45 and 50
This is where **Mark Broadie** joins the team.

I mentioned early on that one of my favourite golf books is "Every Shot Counts" by **Mark Broadie**, who devised the Strokes Gained statistics used on the PGA Tour. Thanks to the Shotlink system, every player can now see exactly how good he is at driving, iron play, wedges, short game, bunker shots and putting. More importantly, he can see where he ranks versus the best in the world. It is truly a *brilliant* use of data. Knowing your numbers can really help identify areas to work on and improve, particularly for tour pros who are looking for marginal gains in skills that are already excellent.

Unfortunately, I am not just a numbers guy. I am a *lazy* numbers guy. At this point, I would like to have been able to show you my Strokes Gained analysis for that decade, highlighting how adept I became in every department of the game. Sadly, I am not on the PGA tour, so nobody is storing this data for me. I never kept a proper record for myself, or at least not enough to bear the scrutiny of the data police.

Here is my estimate of how those 6 shots broke down:

Department	Handicap	Highlight
Driving	+1	I removed the scoop and sway in my swing
Approach Play	+1	My irons also improved because of this
Short Game	+1	Better bunker play and chipping
Age Related	-1	I got older and weaker. I hit the ball less far
Putting	+4	I did all the things I will talk about later
Total	+6	My handicap went from 5 to +1

Hopelessly imprecise numbers. Bernhard would not be impressed.

Mark Broadie will tell you quite categorically that if you can hit the ball further you will improve your scores (provided you retain your accuracy). Bryson de Chambeau has worked this one out too. Conversely, as you get older, the ball flies less far and your scores will increase. That explains the age-related number.

Scientific research (The Yips, Smith et al, 2000) suggests that the putting yips increase 18-hole scores by an average of 4.5 putts per round on average. My putting improved by about 4 shots, which is in the same ballpark. **Can we conclude therefore that I no longer had the yips?**

It looks quite compelling, doesn't it? I love data, even when it is slightly flaky like this.

That is more than enough blowing of my rather small trumpet. You now have all the information to decide for yourself.

It is worth reiterating at this point that **I am still not a great putter**. It is still frequently the worst part of my game. My friends (I do have a few nowadays) would tell you I am not even a *good* putter. By my own definition, I am on the cusp between Normal and Nervous. My average hovers around 30 putts per round, which is nowhere near the top guys. The best players on tour are below 28, although this statistic is *not* the most reliable determinant of good putting. Strokes Gained Putting is.

What I am, however, is someone whose love of the game has returned. If it is possible for a middle-aged golfer like me to get over the yips and even occasionally compete with (or more accurately, lose to) top amateurs and seasoned professionals, then it is definitely possible for you to turn things around too.

(I didn't want to interrupt the flow back there, but that scientific reference "Smith et al" got me wondering. Who is this "al" guy? He seems to have got his name on about half of the world's research publications. He must be very intelligent, and definitely not lazy. He should get a Nobel prize. Maybe he should be my new hero. Maybe *he* is actually a *she* and called Alison. It is about time a few more women got Nobel Prizes)

Photographic Evidence

If you're still wavering about my credentials, here is some heavily doctored footage. It is amazing what you can do with Photoshop.

SENIOR OPEN CHAMPIONSHIP, CARNOUSTIE: 2016

Rocking the pencil grip. I think I missed this one. Look carefully in the background close to my ever-so-still head and you will spot the main man himself, Bernhard Langer. It is as close as I have ever been to him physically. Mentally, we've been much closer at times. I think that is Jean Van de Velde on the right. Things did not go well for him on the 18th hole that year either.

SENIOR OPEN CHAMPIONSHIP, CARNOUSTIE: 2016

Tom Watson and me. Just two old guys hitting balls on the range. I was so nervous, I spent most of my time behind the ball, pretending to practice my Jason Day visualisation technique, thereby avoiding having to hit it. Tom was shaping 3-woods at a marker post as if it were the easiest thing in the world. If this picture included sound, it would be dominated by the thud of Sandy Lyle obliterating balls with his 7 iron just out of shot to the right.

SENIOR OPEN CHAMPIONSHIP, CARNOUSTIE: 2016

I was incapable of speech at this point, and may possibly have wet myself. I doubt Tom has any recollection of this seminal moment in my life.

FINAL OF THE PRESIDENT'S PUTTER, RYE, 2017

PHOTOGRAPH © COPYRIGHT EDWARD WEBB

I did hole this nasty 5-footer, but 4 holes later I was shaking hands with the winner, Will Dugdale.

FINAL QUALIFYING: THE OPEN CHAMPIONSHIP. ROYAL CINQUE PORTS (DEAL), 2017

This is before teeing off in the afternoon. My face is conveniently in shadow, but it really is me. I had already shot 79 that morning, so my hopes weren't high. Things did not improve, but like Humphrey Bogart and Ingrid Bergman in Casablanca, I'll always have Zander.

CHAPTER

5

WHAT IS YOUR PUTTING HANDICAP?

"HE HAS A DECENT LONG GAME, BUT PUTTS LIKE A 36 HANDICAPPER"
You've probably heard this (or said it) about someone with putting troubles. It might even have been said about you. It certainly has been said about me.

The Strokes Gained analysis is the best way to assess your game, but what about something more intuitive? What would your Putting Handicap be?

Let's remind ourselves about the key components of the game:

Driving
Approach Play
Short Game
Putting

Your handicap is your blended ability at each of those skills. But which is the most important?

If you do the maths, you will find that 40-45% of your shots are putts. But actually, many of them are tap-ins that require no skill, even for a yipper. So, **40% is too high** an estimate for putting's contribution to your handicap.

With the help of Mark Broadie, Shotlink and the PGA tour, the R&A/USGA have recently published their "Distance Insights Report", which addresses the question of whether the modern ball travels too far. 100 pages of data. For me, that's like reading Shakespeare.

In trying to answer that question, they have calculated the extent to which driving, approach play, short game and putting contribute to success on Tour. The numbers are as follows:

Driving	29%	On the increase recently, which is their concern
Approach Play	32%	Reducing recently
Short Game	18%	Reducing recently
Putting	21%	Stable

These are the contribution to success for tour players and may not be perfect for you and me, but they are a decent estimate. We will use them.

4 HANDICAPS INSTEAD OF 1

Using the numbers above, if you had four separate handicaps, one for each component of the game, here is how they would relate to your actual handicap.

Actual Handicap *Equals*

	29% of	Driving Handicap
Plus	32% of	Approach Handicap
Plus	18% of	Short Game Handicap
Plus	21% of	Putting Handicap

Mathematically (and removing the word "handicap" to make it clearer),

> *Actual = 29% Driving + 32% Approach + 18% Short Game + 21% Putting*

What we care about is Putting, so we will flip this equation around as follows:

$$Putting = \frac{Actual - (29\%\ Driving + 32\%\ Approach + 18\%\ Short\ Game)}{0.21}$$

As an example, Let's take my handicap during the Lost Decades:

5.4	Actual Handicap:	My handicap was pretty stable
0.0	Driving:	It has always been the best part of my game
1.0	Approach:	My irons were pretty good then too
5.0	Short Game:	I wasn't great in bunkers and my chipping needed work

That would imply my Putting handicap was as follows:

$$Putting = \frac{5.4 - (29\% \times Zero + 32\% \times 1 + 18\% \times 5)}{0.21} = 20$$

So, at my worst, I was putting like a 20 handicapper

Do the same calculation for yourself.

Be honest. Identifying your weaknesses is the first step to removing them. Ask Mark Broadie, or every pro on the PGA tour.

Even if, like me, you can't do a PGA Strokes Gained analysis on your game, you can do this. Go to www.scaryputter.com and download the spreadsheet.

(Incidentally, you may now be able to do strokes gained analysis using the new sensors that go into the end of your grips, or using a database like Mark Broadie's GolfMetric app or GolfDataLab).

Science Corner

I like this stuff, so I have done the same analysis for my entire golfing life. Here it is:

| Era | Age | HANDICAP | | | | |
| | | 100% | 29% | 32% | 18% | 21% |
		Actual	**Driving**	**Approach**	**Short Game**	**Putting**
Early Years	13	10	17	12	7	Scratch
	14	8	12	10	6	1
	15	6	6	9	5	2
	16	5	5	5	5	5
	17	5	4	4	5	8
	18	5	3	3	5	11
	19	5	2	2	5	14
	20	5	1	1	5	17
	21	5	1	1	5	17
Lost Decades	22 to 44	5	0	1	5	20
"Glory" Years	45	5	Plus 1	1	5	19
	46	4	Plus 1	1	4	16
	47	3	Plus 1	0	3	13
	48	1	Plus 2	Plus 1	3	6
	49	0	Plus 3	Plus 2	3	5
	50 to 55	Plus 1	Plus 4	Plus 3	2	3

Hopefully, the colour coding helps show what was going on:

Driving: Once I became strong enough, I was always good at this
Approach: Not as good as driving, but I hit my irons well now
Short Game: Once I worked out how to get out of bunkers and chip,
I improved a bit
Putting: A rollercoaster. Maybe 3 today is too generous

CONFIRMATION

In the last chapter I channelled my inner Mark Broadie and estimated that putting contributed 4 strokes to my overall improvement from the dark days of the Lost Decades. Let's take the numbers in the table above and compare to my previous guesses.

	HANDICAP				
	100%	29%	32%	18%	21%
	Actual	**Driving**	**Approach**	**Short Game**	**Putting**
Handicap Change	6.4	4.0	3.5	3.0	17.0
Strokes Gained	6.4	1.2	1.1	0.5	3.6
Chapter 4 numbers	6.0	0.5	0.5	1.0	4.0

The strokes gained number is the handicap change multiplied by the weighting. I have allocated the 1-stroke distance loss in chapter 4 equally to Driving and Approach.

The numbers are similar, confirming my instinct that from the low point my putting contributed around 4 strokes to the overall improvement of 6.

This table also reminds me that short game and putting are still the areas I can improve the most, and are the ones I should be working on.

Pseudo-Science Alert: Don't take these numbers as precision. 21% for putting is only an assumption, so everything that follows it will be imprecise. However, even if we used say 25%, the shape of the results would be very similar. The useful part of the analysis is to see the *evolution* of the comparative numbers, not the data itself.

CHAPTER

WHAT ARE THE YIPS?

You are probably familiar with the effects of this scourge of humankind, but perhaps you are also completely unfamiliar with its causes. My definition of the yips is something along the lines of:

"an inability to control the putter at impact due to involuntary muscle spasms"

It is hardly a snappy definition. It doesn't even begin to cover the destructive nature of the yips, but it covers everything we need to fix them.

YIPS AREN'T JUST FOR PUTTING

For the sake of completeness, I think I should note at this point that although the golfing yips occur mostly with putting, they do occasionally break out in chipping or even in the long game (like with Hank Haney). You may have occasionally spotted a poor soul whose knees collapse at impact whilst driving the ball. This is probably a distant cousin of the putter yip. Strangely, these unusual strains of the virus do not necessarily appear in those who struggle with putting, and vice versa. Very odd, but that goes beyond the scope or courage of this book, and I am relieved to say I have never suffered myself. Suffice it to say that some of the characteristics and fixes are probably similar.

IT'S NOT JUST A GOLF THING

Golf is not the only sport in which the yips can surface. We have shared the love with a few others. Some of you may remember world darts champion Eric Bristowe, the "Crafty Cockney". Late in his career, Eric suffered from "dartitis", the inability to release his darts, undoubtedly due to a variation of the same syndrome. Snooker players and baseball pitchers have also been known to suffer, as have professional violinists and pianists. I am living proof of this transferability of the yips. In my darker moments, they afflicted me equally when I tried to hit a table-tennis forehand or bowl a cricket ball. What all these have in common is the breakdown of a heavily repeated action.

WHAT CAUSES THE YIPS?

Is it a result of a weak mind (as many non-yippers will assert), is it a genetic disorder, is it a contagious disease, is it an alien infection? Who knows? I am not sure anybody really does, and I'm generally suspicious of anyone who claims to. The safest thing we can probably say is that the yips result from a combination of factors; social, physical, neurological, mental, situational.

However, here are a few specific things that most golfers know:|

- Kids typically don't yip whilst "experienced" golfers are more prone to it.
- The yips are more likely to make an appearance on putts that matter (perhaps more accurately, putts that we think matter. None of them really matter, but that is another chapter).
- They occur more frequently on short putts, and under competitive pressure.
- They tend to occur at the moment of impact, not on the backswing.

SCIENTIFIC RESEARCH

There is actually quite a lot out there. If you search for yips on www.pubmed.gov you will find many pieces of serious research. Perhaps a simpler solution is to read the excellent summary "The Science of the Yips" (Robert E. Wharen, Debbie J. Crews, and Charles H. Adler) in the Routledge International Handbook of Golf Science, my new favourite golf book.

I am intentionally not going to go through any of the research in detail, not least because I can't legitimately claim to have read or understood it all. There are plenty of words I am not familiar with. The numbers I am more comfortable with, and my layman's summary is that the scientific community has not yet reached a consensus on how to define the yips or its causes.

However, there is some evidence that the yips are more likely to occur in people to whom the following terms might apply: analytical, serious, perfectionist, self-conscious. Maybe some of that explains how they managed to infect me.

ARE THE YIPS A PHYSICAL PROBLEM OR A MENTAL PROBLEM?

There is scientific debate as to whether the yips are a result of focal dystonia (a neurological, physical condition), or psychological anxiety, or possibly a combination of both.

Some of the scientists like to put yippers in 2 categories:

- Type I, who have physical, neurological problems, and
- Type II, who have mental anxiety problems (they rather charmingly call them "chokers")

I have read the research, and I can't tell you if I am a Type I or a Type II yipper, so my view is to leave those definitions well alone.

However, that distinction between neurological and psychological problems is important. Let's look briefly at the neurological part of things:

Focal dystonia is what happens when the neural pathways we use for a particular movement can break down after a large number of repetitions.

WHAT IS A NEURAL PATHWAY?
In order to execute a putting stroke, your entire body is coordinated through a particular route in your nervous system, connecting your brain, eyes and body. That specific combination of nerves is called a neural pathway. The argument is that it basically wears out and misfires after too many repetitions. It is a physical problem with the nervous system and has little if anything to do with anxiety.

When that neural pathway is broken, the solution is not to patch it up but to create a shiny, brand-new one instead. This all makes sense to me, and in the absence of any more plausible theory it is the one I subscribe to, enabling me to draw the following conclusion:

The yips are a neurological (i.e. physical) condition, not a psychological one

This sweeping statement is a vast oversimplification, and I am sure a neurologist would have a great deal to say about it. Luckily, I am not a neurologist so I can continue blithely with my assumption. For what it's worth, Hank Haney would probably agree with me (he's not a neurologist either).

Don't get me wrong; yippers have plenty of psychological issues too, but they are largely a consequence of the neurological problem.

Here is how I would classify our groups of golfers according to their neurological and psychological problems:

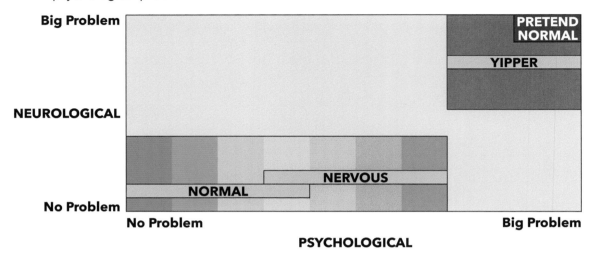

Normal and Nervous golfers have primarily psychological issues, if at all. Yippers have *both* psychological *and* neurological issues and curing them requires fixing both problems.

The neurological problem with yips cannot be fixed through the mental game alone.

So, if you want to fix the yips, you need to create a new neural pathway:

You Need to Change Something: Big Time

Perhaps this is no surprise, as we have already drawn this conclusion with my groundbreaking Victoria Falls analogy.

Here is a well-known quotation, usually attributed to Albert Einstein:

"The definition of insanity is doing the same thing over and over again and expecting different results"

There is some doubt as to whether Albert really said this, and significantly more doubt as to whether he was talking about golf, but it delivers a perfect message for yippers, particularly those pretending to be Normal. If you want to eradicate the yips from your game, you must do something radically different.

But how on earth do you identify the right changes to make that happen? There are thousands of things you could try, and how do you know which of them will create a new neural pathway, and how long will *that* one last?

DO YOU HAVE A "YIP SIGNATURE"?

If you have the yips, the first thing you will need to do is perhaps counterintuitive.

You need to become *more* familiar (not less familiar) with your yips.

In order to fix them, you need to understand them better, and identify more closely what really is going on.

A few years ago, a friend of mine who had suffered (and thankfully survived) a heart attack told me that apparently everybody has their own individual heart attack "signature". By that, he meant that some people feel tightness in the chest, others pain in the left arm, others struggle to breathe. Everybody feels and recognises a heart attack in a slightly different way. I believe the same is true with the yips.

My yips may not be the same as your yips.

Going back to our definition, the key question is "which muscles are going into spasm?".

Quite why these muscles are doing it I will leave to the scientists, but let's try to narrow down the potential culprits. Very few people suffer from "big muscle" yips. I have never heard of involuntary buttock-clenching on the greens, or at least if I have, it was more related to the previous night's food and drink. Conversely, I am unaware of any "finger yippers". In most of the cases I have seen, experienced or heard about, the wrists have been the weak link.

This is where we address the critical task of identifying your "yip signature".

WHAT IS MY YIP SIGNATURE?

For me, the danger has always come from the right wrist. I am one of those strange people who write with their left hand but play sports right-handed (my family will not forgive me if I fail to say at this point that I am amphibious). As a child I played a fair amount of right-handed table tennis (when I wasn't using the ball for chipping practice) and other racquet sports. Does that mean I have blown a fuse in my right-handed neural pathway? I have no idea, but for sure the right wrist has been providing that extra snap in my putting stroke just when I least needed it. My left hand in contrast is relatively sedate, lazy even (like the rest of me).

You may be unsure about your "yip signature" and I can understand why. You may not even have one. The whole yip thing happens so quickly that it is quite difficult to analyse what happened. However, identifying the bad hand is the first step in fixing the problem.

HERE'S HOW YOU DO IT:

Try putting with only the left hand. Don't bother with a target, just try stroking the ball. Does it feel nice and secure or horribly sketchy?

Now try it with only the right hand. One will feel better than the other. If you are unlucky maybe both will be bad, but the key is just to identify. If neither feels dodgy you may need to add a bit of pressure to the situation until something snaps. Add a target, have a putting contest, do it on the course, until eventually the yip shows its ugly face.

It should not take long before you have a clear idea of where your weakness lies. I am trying not to lead the witness here, but there is some evidence to suggest that the focal dystonia typically occurs in the *dominant* hand. However, when you are a bit mixed up like me, the dominant hand may not be so easy to spot.

At this point I suggest you go and try this now. If not now, then certainly before you read the chapter on how to hold the club. It will be far less relevant and barely worth reading if you haven't done your homework.

WHAT IS BERNHARD'S YIP SIGNATURE?

I feel compelled to ask this question, but it has been troubling me.

It is not always easy to guess people's problems from the way they putt. Look at Matt Kuchar. Weird setup. I am willing to bet he has no problems whatsoever; he just likes putting like that. The same goes for Tommy Fleetwood and Alex Noren. If you cannot reliably tell by looking at someone whether they have any putting problems, how can you pretend to know what their yip signature is?

In a way, it confirms the point I was making about other people offering you advice. I don't know how Bernhard feels, and it is both difficult and wrong for me to speculate about it. He has also gone through so many iterations that he may even have had more than one signature problem. He is a (very) professional golfer and probably hits thousands of putts every week. That's more than enough repetitions to burn through any number of neural pathways.

That may sound like a cop-out, but we will return to the subject. Let's stick to what we can actually feel ourselves.

WHAT IS THE TYPICAL YIP SIGNATURE?

Thanks here to Christian Marquardt, neuroscientist and founder of SAM PuttLab. Here are the typical results of his extensive testing of many yippers. Imagine we are doing the one-handed test for both hands, and testing both forehand and backhand (i.e., opposite directions) for each hand.

Left hand forehand:	No yip	✔
Left hand backhand:	No yip	✔
Right hand forehand:	Yip	✘
Right hand backhand:	No yip	✔

Almost invariably, it is the forehand of the dominant right hand that is the problem, but intriguingly there rarely seems any problem if yippers turn around and try a right-handed backhand.

WHAT IS YOUR YIP SIGNATURE?

Firstly, if you find that neither hand has a problem, Congratulations! You don't have the yips, at least not by my definition of them. Just relax and enjoy the remainder of the book, picking up preventive tips on the way so that you never have to endure them in the future.

If your right hand is the problem, then join the club. Ride with me towards the sunlit uplands of golfing heaven, knowing that I am your long-lost twin. Because the prevalent hand for the yips is the dominant one, you have plenty of company.

If it's your left hand, then it would be inconsistent, arrogant and hypocritical of me to claim I know *exactly* how it feels. It's more like I'm your cousin. We are family, but we don't understand each other quite so well. It will not exactly be a case of reversing polarity, but you should try with your left hand a variation of all the suggestions I will make for the right. You will need to experiment more, but everything else remains the same. We're still on the same journey. I am with you, just on a different horse.

55

If it's both hands, or neither, or something different (I would love to know what: please tell me if it's the buttocks), then it's like we're just reasonably well acquainted. You will have to do much more of the heavy lifting. I will still be the wise guru, showing you the path to enlightenment but not actually joining you on the journey. I will pop in from time to time to see how you're getting on, a little like Gandalf in Lord of the Rings.

Now that you have identified your own yip signature, you are ready. I will permit you to continue reading and start the road to recovery (or the "Springboard to Victory", as a friend of mine likes to call it when he is 3 down in matchplay). The key to it all is to isolate and exclude the part of your body that is misbehaving.

CHAPTER

DEALING WITH PUTTER NERVES

We all know golfers out there with an unusual approach to putting. Some are just unusual people. I like unusual people – they make up for my lack of Seve sparkle – but most people with a weird putting style have it because they are struggling, and a fair subset of those have full-blown yips.

Here are a few popular approaches I have seen or attempted. They are not all necessarily *anti-yip* strategies, just things people do to deal with nerves. They have a wide range of success and failure. Some are fatuously stupid ideas, but I have watched otherwise extremely intelligent people attempt them. Very few address the key yip signature problem. I will give each method a score out of 10 for its effectiveness. It is merely *my* score. You may find them more or less useful than me, but just remember, change for change's sake can help in the short term but is unlikely to be the long-term answer. **Change needs to be *targeted*.**

SURPRISE: Sneak up on the ball while it is not expecting it, preferably from a downwind position so it can't smell you either. Hit the ball before it knows what is happening, and hopefully you will have completed the stroke before the yips can get involved.

1/10 This never worked for me. I've never seen it work for anyone. The problem of course is that you cannot fool your own mind. Certainly not this way. The yips will win this race.

STATUES: Stand calmly over the ball for as long as it takes until you are 100% comfortable to hit it. Then you can just go ahead and give it a carefree stroke.

1/10 This never works. You are never 100% comfortable. You will freeze and the yips will outwait you.

CHECKLIST CHARLIE: A more systematic version of Statues. This player has a checklist of 17 things to confirm before he swings, and 23 more during the stroke. If you consciously follow the sequence, all will be well.

1/10 I know a few Checklist Charlies. They use it for the long game too. You could go and have a cup of tea while they're doing their pre-shot routines. You might need something stronger. When you are swinging the club, you should allow yourself only one thought, possibly two if you are really pushing it. Checklists are for when you are practicing.

THE TOE-POKE: Address the ball normally, then rotate the putter head through 90 degrees anti-clockwise so the toe of the putter is next to the ball. Toe-poke it.

1/10 I watched this happen in a national event. After the round, I asked what was going on, and my playing partner told me that he knew he would miss the putt using his normal putting stroke, so he was giving it a go with that one instead. Finally, I had met someone with bigger issues than me. Please never try this unless you have a blade putter, your ball is right up against the fringe of the green, and you need to hit down on it.

WHITE KNUCKLES: Grip the club so tightly that there is no possibility of any muscles twitching. They are already at maximum effort, so you are perfectly safe. Maintain this pressure throughout the stroke.

1/10 I have had the misfortune to observe this technique hundreds of times close up. Even standing at a safe distance it is scary. It usually ends up with some kind of seizure or hypoxia. Of all the techniques here, I couldn't recommend it less.

THE BIG EASY: Here the idea is to have such a long, easy stroke that it requires no acceleration at the ball and therefore no hit and no yip.

2/10 Ernie Els has a long, easy backswing in his long game. It is a thing of beauty. He used to putt like that too before it all became a little twitchy. He then channelled his inner Bernhard, switched to a belly putter, and won another Open Championship (at my home track Lytham). Amazing. A long slow backswing provides too much opportunity for a decelerative yip followed by the much-loved double-hit. No.

THE TRIGGER: Take the club back a truly short distance (ideally no more than 2 inches) and accelerate hard through the ball. There is then no chance of a deceleration and the clubhead has no time to deviate from its correct alignment.

2/10 I know people who do this. Occasionally they putt quite well, but it looks terrifying and they putt badly much more frequently. Maybe it helps with direction on short putts (although I question this), but distance control is almost impossible. Don't do it. It is not a fix.

ALCOHOL: Have a few drinks before (or even during) your game. You will care less about putting and will consequently putt better.

3/10 Some friends of mine rely on this heavily. I am not going to recommend it wholeheartedly, but the post-lunch liqueur kummel is not known as the "putting mixture" for nothing. Other alcohol is available and works in a similar fashion. It may well help on those tricky short putts, but this will be offset by the damage it does to your long game, decision-making and liver. This is not the answer but perversely it does identify the putting benefits of caring less.

DRUGS: Take a few beta blockers before you play, or maybe even something stronger.

?/10 I don't know much about this one. Beta blockers have been around for decades and supposedly suppress nerves. Whether they have ever been used successfully on tour is a matter of debate but, if they really worked, I suspect the cat would be out of the bag by now. There has been research suggesting that Botox injections can reduce the effect of the yips, but it is neither conclusive nor scientifically tested as to its effects on other parts of your body or golf game. I would never try or recommend this. Recreational drugs of any type are unlikely to help your score.

BELLY WEDGE: Take out your wedge with the straightest bottom line (lob wedges are often a bit rounded), address the ball with that edge level with the middle of the ball, and thin it at the hole.

5/10 Bizarrely, this worked quite well for me. I still do it occasionally when the ball is just in the fringe around the green. For some reason, the added difficulty of making contact at the ball's equator with a sharp leading edge seems to distract the yips. I can't explain it. It's not a practical putting solution though. Long putts with a belly wedge will not work well.

CLOSE YOUR EYES: Go through your pre-shot routine as normal. Take up your address position, close your eyes and visualise the hole as you make your stroke. Trust your body. Because you are not looking at the ball, you will not see or worry about the impact.

5/10 If you've never tried this, you might think it madness, but it is not as bad as you might think. Sergio Garcia has recently revealed that he did this during his Masters victory. It takes a lot of trust, and it becomes a liability for longer putts, but it can help. It's great as a practice routine because it removes impact from your consciousness. Yippers worry about what happens at impact. If they don't see it, they will worry less.

LOOK AT THE HOLE: Align yourself normally in your address position, then tilt your head to look at the hole and make your stroke whilst continuing to look at the hole. This connects you mentally to your target and away from what your hands are doing.

6/10 Jordan Spieth did this when he was the best putter in the world, so that's quite a recommendation. However, he no longer does it and neither do any of his fellow pros. This is perhaps better than closing the eyes and can really help on short putts. Worth trying as part of an overall solution, but I don't think it is a proper fix on its own.

CONTROL YOUR BREATHING: Practice yoga-style breathing exercises to control your heart rate and lower your levels of anxiety. Concentrating on your breathing will also divert attention from the nonsense in your head.

6/10 I have tried this, rather half-heartedly. My attempts at yoga have generally been more targeted at flexibility, which is another Achilles' heel of mine. I am usually in so much pain that breathing control goes out of the window. It's probably a decent idea and worth exploring further.

RED DOT: No, not the red dots behind the eyes of the White-Knuckle specialist as his blood vessels begin to haemorrhage. This is the Red Dot that Louis Oosthuizen put on his glove when he won The Open at St Andrews. The remarkably successful idea was that as soon as he saw the red dot, he knew he had to give 100% concentration. When he took the glove off again, he could relax.

6/10 He won The Open using it. It definitely allowed him to stick to the plan and focus at the right times, although strictly he used it for the long game, not putting.

On an entirely different subject, "Pale Blue Dot" is one of my favourite things ever. A picture of Earth from 6 billion kilometres away. The commentary about it by another of my heroes – the astronomer Carl Sagan – is poetic in its beauty, and required listening for anyone who needs reminding we are all the same.

CHANGE YOUR PUTTER: This is often the first thing people try. It's tempting. We have all done it. I have a bagful of putters that bear testament to this.

7/10 It can help, but usually it doesn't, and rarely is it the complete answer. However, equipment is a vital part of the equation, so it merits a chapter of its own.

THE RHYTHM METHOD: Establish an automatic, subconscious routine to your setup and stroke. Whatever that may be, make the same movements every time so that the whole process always takes the same amount of time.

9/10 A really good idea. Following a routine can stop you thinking, and that is a good thing. Some of my best putting has been when I followed the same routine, irrespective of the type of putt or pressure involved. More on this later.

PERPETUAL MOTION: Here the idea is to keep the clubhead moving at all times. That way you will never freeze over the ball. Practice strokes should move seamlessly into address, which moves seamlessly into the stroke itself. Look at Brandt Snedeker's routine; the clubhead is always moving.

9/10 Again, I like this. Putting is a closed task that you must initiate yourself. By keeping everything moving it feels like you are being more reactive, closer to a tennis player during a rally. Once the clubhead stops moving, pressure begins to build in your head.

CHANGE YOUR GRIP: Change the way you hold the club and use a new neural pathway.

10/10 This is the most important one. So important that it is also going to get a chapter all of its own.

CHANGE YOUR MENTAL GAME: We know putting is 90% mental, and that the other 10% might be mental as well. Man up, and sort yourself out.

10/10 The End Game. The mental game is everything in putting, but it is not as simple as manning up, particularly if you are a woman. Finding a way to change from quivering wreck to confident putter requires another chapter. Quite a big one.

HARRY POTTER: Fashion a putter out of thousand-year-old cherry wood with a unicorn hair core. Wear a gown and a pair of round glasses and shout "Yippus Expelliamus!" as loudly as you can during your stroke. If that doesn't work, then go all-in and give it the full killing curse "Avada Focus Dystonius Kedavra".

0/10 OK. I made this one up.

STAR WARS: Use the Force:

0/10 Recommend it I don't.

CHAPTER

MINIMISING YIP POTENTIAL

Let's go all the way back to Chapter 7 for a recap.
"Once you have identified your yip signature, you can now start the road to recovery".

CHANGING YOUR GRIP DIRECTLY ADDRESSES
THE NEUROLOGICAL PROBLEM OF THE YIPS

Changing your grip is the first -and hardest – few miles (sorry Bernhard, the first 7.83972 kilometres) of that road. By switching to something radically different (and probably initially uncomfortable), you will stop using the old, broken neural pathway and start building a new one.

However, before we get going on that, we need to do some more science and introduce the concept of **"Yip Potential"**

MINIMISE THE YIP POTENTIAL

We are all different. For me, a yip manifests itself as a twitch of the right hand. Specifically, an unconscious, uncontrolled movement through of the right hand as if I were hitting a greenside bunker shot. Not helpful when you're trying to hole a 2-footer.

HIGH YIP POTENTIAL

Position A   Position B

Take a look at the two pictures above.

My yip signature involved my right hand moving from Position A to Position B at something approaching the speed of light. If only I could somehow trigger it with the driver, I could become a Long Drive Champ.

Look more closely. Beyond the fact that the stroke may be using a broken neural pathway, there are 2 additional problems:

1. There is a lot of play in the wrist. It moves through maybe 120 degrees.
2. Not only can it move a long way, but it is being driven by the power muscles in my forearm.

These are both bad things. They compound the problem. I can give the ball a reasonable hit with my wrist in this position. Sadly, that also means that if the yips get involved, they can have a pretty large (i.e. devastating) effect. If things go wrong, they will go horribly wrong. There is a lot of what we shall call "Yip Potential".

LOW YIP POTENTIAL

Position C

Position D

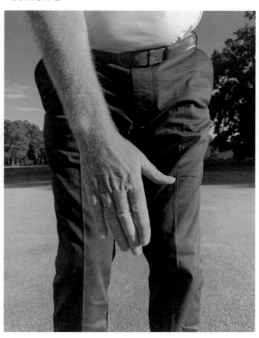

Now look at the next two pictures. If I rotate my forearm by a quarter turn and place my hand on top of the putter shaft (position C), my wrist can't really get involved. It's kind of locked there. It can only move about 30 degrees. It certainly cannot get past position D (I was trying really hard). This movement is also powered by completely different muscles, triggered by different nerves in my forearm. They are tiny muscles too, so they are unable to provide unwanted power.

If we compare the Yip Potential of this second right-hand position (Position C) versus the first one (Position A), we get the following:

The distance the wrist can move A to B is about **4 times** that from C to D.
The muscles powering the move from A to B are at least **2 times** stronger than C to D.
4 x 2 = 8 (this is perhaps the only piece of undeniably rigorous maths in the book)

The power I can produce with my wrist in this position is perhaps one eighth of that in the original position. Consequently, any yip will also only have one eighth of the strength too.

We have just reduced the effect of a yip by a factor of 8.
It is obvious that I should think about changing my grip.

Yes, I know. Putting is an art form not a science. The great putters are all artists. I'm just trying to let science help you improve the odds. You may not be Katniss Everdeen, but you might as well make sure the odds are ever in your favour. I am not suggesting you think about science on the course. Even Bryson doesn't do that.

We have now reached the least interesting but most important phrase in this book.

Your best chance of controlling the yips is by choosing a Low Yip Potential wrist position.

Science Corner

If you are not mathematically minded, I would skip the next couple of pages. If you are, then welcome to my world.

If there were a formula for Yip Potential ("YP) it would be as follows:

Yip Potential = Muscle Strength x Wrist Movement

You multiply the force (in this case muscle strength) by distance (how far the wrist can move).

This is a direct corollary of the schoolboy physics formula:

$$P = M \times g \times h$$

This defines the potential energy of a mass raised above a surface. It essentially describes the amount of energy that something will have by the time it contacts the surface. This potential energy is the equivalent of how bad your yip can be.

Let's imagine the object is a golf ball, and we are dropping it into water.

M   is the mass of the ball
g   is the force being applied to it, the earth's gravitational pull

h   is the height above ground

When the ball lands in the water, it will make a splash, the size of which corresponds to its energy. In the formula, the splash is P and is the equivalent of your yip. Bigger P, bigger splash, bigger yip.

How can you make the splash/yip smaller?

1. Make the ball lighter:
   You can't do this. The R&A and USGA won't let you
2. Drop the ball from a lower height:
   That works. It's the equivalent of a grip position with less play in the wrist
3. Reduce gravity:
   Do the experiment on the moon

This may not be the most practical example I have ever used, but if you did go to the moon, the splash would indeed be less because the force acting on the ball is lower. More practically, this is exactly the equivalent of you taking your stronger wrist muscles out of play.

Pseudo-Science Alert: If you are a rigorous physicist, you will pick all sorts of holes in this. Albert Einstein would not totally approve. It's hardly the General Theory of Relativity but it does broadly make sense. An engineer would think it's OK. It does the job. I would defend it stoutly.

But we are golfers and we do not care about academic rigour. We care about putting.

The last thing you want is for there to be lots of energy available to be put into your yip, so:

The target is to minimise Yip Potential. Am I sounding like Bryson yet?

10

WHAT GRIP SHOULD YOU USE?

When I was learning the game, everybody basically used the same grip. Many just used their long game grip, and most of the rest had progressed to the Reverse Overlap, but not beyond. Left hand below right was considered a ground-breaking innovation. I fondly remember watching a live clip of Tony Jacklin demonstrating it as a radical new technique and promptly missing a 6-footer by a large margin. I found it terrifically funny at the time. Presumably, I was very young; it would have seemed far less amusing by the time I was 21.

RESULTS ARE EVERYTHING, NOT APPEARANCES.
Nowadays, plenty of different grips are used on tour and at your local club, but even now there is still a *stigma* attached to some of them. Ignore that.

PRIDE WILL NOT HELP YOU
Yes, I'm looking at you, Mr Pretend Normal. You are a yipper. Accept it, and move on to fixing it. You are too proud to let people see you with a new grip. You don't want them to label you as weak. They probably do already. We are all weak, but some of us are trying to get stronger. There is no shame in trying anything that will work. Bernhard has shown us this.

YOUR GRIP SHOULD BE RADICALLY DIFFERENT
Remember, you are trying to create an entirely new neural pathway. There is no point switching from a reverse overlap grip to a 10-finger grip. It is just not a big enough change.

69

YOUR GRIP SHOULD MINIMISE YOUR YIP POTENTIAL

The best grip for you will be the one that minimises wrist movement of your problem hand whilst still allowing some feel (without which putting will always be a challenge).

The choice of grip co-mingles with the choice of putter, but here are some of the options and my opinion of how effective they are for me. I will resist giving each a score as I don't know exactly what your yip signature is, so some may work better for you than me.

This is where *you* start to take control. Find the one that works for you. Minimise the amount your bad wrist can move. Ideally, get different, weaker wrist muscles involved.

IT'S GOING TO BE WEIRD

It is important to remember that when you change your grip it will feel odd. That is a good thing. It means it has a decent chance of creating a new neural pathway, thereby kicking the yips into touch. Just make sure that you choose one that suits your particular yip signature. For example, there is little point going left below right if it still exposes your problem hand to the same risk as before. Of course, because the new grip feels odd you may initially lose some feel. It will take some time to acclimatise. Persist. Persevere. Your feel will return.

EXAMPLES OF PUTTING GRIPS

The following photos demonstrate a variety of putting grips with my comments on how they work for me, together with my assessment of how risky they are in terms of Yip Potential. It's not an exhaustive list, although it was quite exhausting trying to impersonate some of the styles. I can't claim to have got the impressions of the pros exactly right, but I hope you get the idea, and by shooting them all at the same time it is perhaps easier to compare the different styles. Clearly, you can find better photos of the genuine articles on the web.

THESE GRIPS ARE NOT JUST FOR YIPPERS

Many perfectly good putters choose to use unconventional grips because they just feel better, or they are trying to limit the effects of Normal nervousness on the golf course.

GRIP TRAFFIC LIGHT SYSTEM
This one is based on Yip Potential

High Yip Potential	Danger. Consider alternatives
Medium Yip Potential	Caution. Worth trying but you can probably do better
Low Yip Potential	Safe. Try this

Pseudo-science Alert: These are my assessments of the grips, based primarily on the way they limit the movement of the right wrist. Please make your own judgement.

"THESE GUYS ARE GOOD"
Most of the players on the PGA tour use the "traditional" putting grips: Reverse Overlap, maybe left below right. i.e. the Red grips above that I am warning against. They don't care about the yips (although they still do get nervous). They are top-end Normal golfers and feel is everything for them. The best guys average around 28 putts per round.

THESE GUYS ARE GOOD TOO
In my opinion, there are also a few Nervous golfers on the PGA tour. Most of them use the low-risk green grips. Do not dismiss them. These guys are still excellent putters. Whatever statistic you choose to use, the difference between the best and worst putters on tour is about 2 shots per round. That is a huge amount when the margins in pro golf are so tight, but even the worst putters with their dodgy grips are averaging below 30 putts per round. You or I would probably trade our putting games for that. These people are the relevant benchmark for the nervous amateur putter.

REVERSE OVERLAP HIGH YIP POTENTIAL

The benchmark grip for good putters. The hands are close together, work together. I think the reason it's called the reverse overlap grip is because the forefinger (and sometimes the middle finger) of the left hand goes over the fingers of the right hand. In the long game, it's the other way round. With a light grip you get excellent feel. Look at Seve Ballesteros in his prime or Patrick Reed today: poetry in motion and I could not be more jealous. This method is **useless** if you have the yips. It is the High Yip Potential position A we used in the example. It is also probably the grip you used while you were developing the yips in the first place. Get away from it.

SPLIT GRIP MEDIUM/HIGH YIP POTENTIAL

Some people find that separating their hands helps. Here is just one example. Apparently, there is an argument that using the hands separately uses a different neural pathway to when they work together. For me, it seemed pretty ineffective.

CRADLE MEDIUM YIP POTENTIAL

This I think has some mileage. The key to it is that by opening up the hands (very weak left hand grip, very strong right hand grip) you end up with your elbows tucked into your sides, supposedly as if you were cradling a baby. Putters are nothing like babies. They are far more badly behaved. Because the elbows are locked, the whole thing feels a bit more secure. The weakness from my perspective is that the wrists still have a fair bit of freedom, but nowhere near as much as in the reverse overlap.

LEFT HAND LOW (CACK-HANDED) MEDIUM/HIGH YIP POTENTIAL

This is now widely used as a standard putting technique. It is also frequently a first stop for golfers looking to control their nerves. I still felt my right hand had a bit of freedom to misbehave, so my method involved getting the right hand really strong and the wrist locked in the "back" position against the shaft, never letting it even get back to neutral. It's the next picture in the series.

JACKO LEFT HAND LOW LOW/MEDIUM YIP POTENTIAL

This is the version I used for a while. My right-hand grip is much stronger than in the standard cack-handed grip. That locks in my right elbow and it all feels more trapped in there. It's getting a bit closer to the Bernhard solution or the grip of Alex Noren without the forward press. It's ugly but you have to choose function over form every time.

JORDAN SPIETH MEDIUM/HIGH YIP POTENTIAL

I don't think I got this quite right. Jordan has his hands so close together (closer than in this picture, anyway) that it is barely left below right. I am still in awe of his putting (even now when he is a shadow of his former brilliance), but for me this has too much room to go wrong.

THE CLAW LOW YIP POTENTIAL

Chris di Marco was the first I know of to do this, with very high hands. Because the right hand sits on top of the shaft, the wrist is not involved at all and it is therefore ideal for my particular weakness. This is essentially the Low Yip Potential Position C from the previous chapter. No surprise that I use it a lot. It also has a few fingers of the right hand involved, so I think it helps to retain feel. I use lowish hands and a straight right arm. It is possible to make this even more extreme, taking the right hand even further over so that the back of the hand is facing the target, effectively making it a backhand stroke for both hands. We know from Christian Marquardt that backhands generally don't yip.

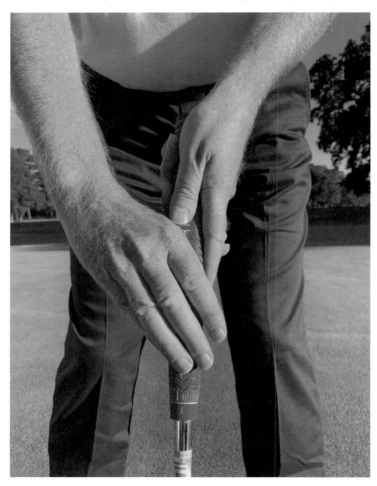

THE PENCIL LOW YIP POTENTIAL

A variation of the claw but with fewer fingers on the grip. This feels a little more natural than the claw and is perhaps better for long putts but maybe worse for the all-important 3 to 6 footers where stability is key. Used frequently by Sergio after binning the belly putter. Definitely a contender. Low Yip Potential and you're never going to white-knuckle this grip.

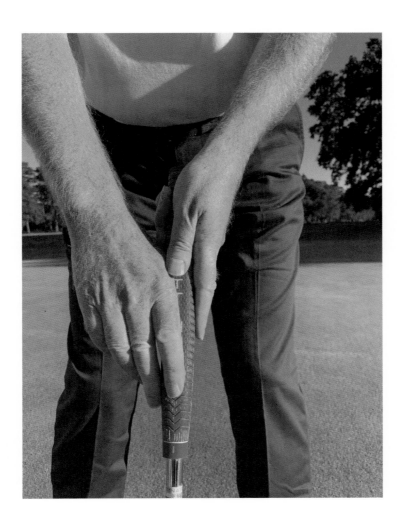

ALEX NOREN LOW/MEDIUM YIP POTENTIAL

Inspired by one of Bernhard's mid-career solutions, Alex has a 10-finger grip and an extreme forward press. I don't believe he has any putting issues at all. His stroke looks fantastic, and by locking in the right hand against his left forearm shaft this stroke looks and feels really secure. You need lots of loft on the putter to get this to work. The follow-through of his stroke is pure hold-off, thereby preventing the right wrist from releasing.

MATT KUCHAR LOW/MEDIUM YIP POTENTIAL

Kooch uses his mid-length armlock putter to devastating effect. He is consistently top 30 on Tour in putting and there is no discernible change in his numbers over the years. He runs the shaft up his left forearm, which is technically not anchoring but adds stability. His right-hand grip is pretty standard i.e. not ideal for me. I tried this but never got much feel on long putts. I suspect that armlock putting may be best on fast greens where you don't need to hit the ball hard. Maybe that's why you see it on Tour but rarely at the local golf club. Again, this requires a specialist club with maybe 7 degrees of loft, as will any armlock method.

WEBB SIMPSON LOW YIP POTENTIAL

A combination of Kuchar's armlock method with the Claw grip in the right hand. Webb's overall game (including his putting) is not particularly pretty but it is highly effective. Combined with a brisk stroke he looks like he will never miss. I rate this method highly. Again, you need a specialist club with extra loft. Webb suffered when his belly putter was taken away from him by the rule change. He fell from consistently around 30th on tour in putting prior to the ban to 174th immediately after it, taking around 1 stroke per round more in the process. With his current technique he has reversed that and more, regaining 1.2 strokes per round and ranking around 5th on tour. For a tour pro those are huge changes.

BRYSON DE CHAMBEAU LOW YIP POTENTIAL

Difficult to show in a single photo but it's an extremely upright version of the Kooch. The shaft is near vertical. It looks very mechanical but that isn't necessarily a bad thing. We're not trying to be Picasso. It's tricky to find a putter set up like this. Definitely worth trying if you can. I greatly admire Bryson's determination to go his own way and his desire to leave no stone unturned. In a way, that reminds me of Bernhard. Bryson is not a yipper, but he likes physics. It is no surprise to me that this is a setup he favours.

TOMMY FLEETWOOD MEDIUM YIP POTENTIAL

Tommy has his right hand completely under the shaft with barely any of it touching the club. It feels really weird to me but keeps the face pretty square. I like Tommy and I like his method (he keeps the fingers of his right hand pointing down but I like this variation). The problem with it for me is that the right wrist remains available to add some unwanted extra oomph.

JACK NICKLAUS MEDIUM/HIGH YIP POTENTIAL

This picture isn't worthy of the great man. Jack Nicklaus was perhaps the greatest pressure putter ever. He had balls of steel. His piston method involved crouching over the ball and pushing his right arm almost horizontally towards the hole. Not bad, but it still leaves my right wrist exposed to misbehaviour. It's unlikely to be a big enough change to help with the yips.

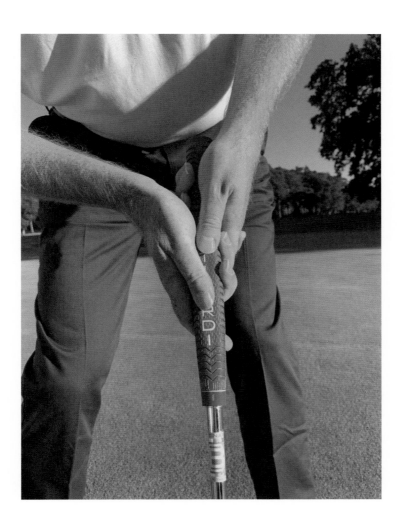

THE BERNHARD LOW YIP POTENTIAL

This was Bernhard's individual mid-career solution, after he had used both the standard grip and left below right. He clamped his left forearm to the shaft using his right hand. It was also the inspiration for Alex Noren's setup. I quite like it. It looks like a solution for someone with the same issues as me.

THE LONG PUTTER LOW/MEDIUM YIP POTENTIAL

Bernhard tried everything. His current long putter method seems to be a keeper and involves holding the grip just away from his chest. His right hand then provides the stroke, but he does still turn his chest. I never found a putter that felt OK for this stroke, either before or after the anchoring ban. For me, the right hand is too exposed, although tellingly Bernhard uses a very unusual right-hand grip in which the shaft actually goes *between* his fingers. Adam Scott uses a similar technique but with a Tommy Fleetwood right hand grip.

MIGUEL ANGEL JIMENEZ MEDIUM YIP POTENTIAL

Miguel seems far too relaxed to suffer from the yips. Maybe it's the Rioja. Despite this, he changes putters all the time and even his grip occasionally. I was shocked to see him the other day using this left below right grip with a *left-hand claw variation*. That's quite something. He shot 8 under par using it during his record breaking 707th appearance on the European Tour. If you have a dodgy left hand, maybe this is the answer. Probably not for me.

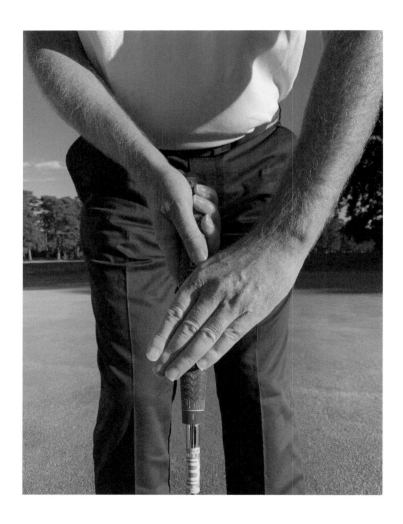

BELLY

Stick the end of the grip against your belly button and that will provide stability to the stroke. This form of anchoring clearly used to help a lot of people, but you can't do it any more because it was banned in 2016. Webb Simpson and Keegan Bradley were notable victims of the rule change. Both struggled to find an alternative method. I tried the belly technique, but to me it seemed like the worst of both worlds; little feel and little safety. Fortunately, the removal of it as a legitimate technique means I don't have to show you a picture of the grip fighting to stay in place whilst embedded in my flabby midriff.

SIDE-SADDLE

Even I am not old enough to remember Sam Snead, but I have always thought of him as a direct golfing ancestor of Ernie Els; effortless power through a beautiful, rhythmic swing, and slightly dodgy on the greens. Sam Snead suffered terribly from the yips, first adopting a croquet-style solution until that was banned, and then inventing his side-saddle approach in which he faced the hole. Very few others have followed suit, although Bryson experimented with it, and I lost a play-off to an American amateur using it. Apparently the USGA weren't happy with Bryson's centre-shafted putter and encouraged him not to use it. I wish they'd had a word with the guy who beat me.

VIJAY SINGH

Vijay still plays amazing golf, but every time I see him on the television he is using a new, increasingly bizarre grip. I'm not going to show you an example because next week it will be different.

LEFT-HANDED PUTTING: THE LAST RESORT

If you get a chance, look at Bob Charles putting. It looks so classy and simple, a perfect pendulum with no wrist action at all. However, in this case I'm not actually suggesting copying his style, but his orientation. How about left-handed putting? *I would only advise doing this if all other avenues are exhausted*, but if you reverse the direction you will almost certainly create a new neural pathway. If ever the yips returned with a vengeance for me, I would putt left-handed. I am a lefty at heart. I love putting that way round but have never got my head round aiming correctly. I simply don't know where I'm pointing. You may fare better. The weirdness level is extremely high for such a dramatic change, so don't be surprised if the acclimatisation process is longer.

HANDS HIGH VERSUS HANDS LOW

By putting "hands high" I mean having the hands relatively far away from the body and the putter shaft close to vertical. Think Steve Stricker or Branden Grace. "Hands low" is where the hands are closer to your knees and the putter shaft is probably more angled. Think Seve Ballesteros or Patrick Reed. It's worth experimenting with this because the feel can be remarkably different.

I always thought that "hands high" was best for me because it seemed a bit more rigid and safer, whilst "hands low" seemed to be riskier. However, recently I have discovered that low hands can feel more natural.

HOW TIGHT SHOULD YOU GRIP IT?

As loosely as you can without losing control of the putter. On a scale of 1 to 10, never more than 2. There are too many white-knuckle putters out there already.

BUT WHAT ABOUT FEEL?

We have already discussed how the putting superstars have beautiful, flowing strokes with soft hands and loads of feel. Brad Faxon, Seve, Patrick Reed, Rickie Fowler. We know that changing grip may initially reduce your feel, but that it will return as your new stroke beds in. However, some of the safe grips I have described (the green Low Yip Potential ones) will always have less feel than the standard reverse overlap grip.

Feel is vital but it is a subjective thing. Choosing your new grip is a *compromise* between feel and safety.

Let's try to put a bit of structure round this. Here is how I score each of the putting grips I have just listed, rated out of 10 for both feel and safety:

Method	Feel	
Reverse Overlap	10	**High Feel**
Jack	9	
Left hand low	8	
Split	7	
Pencil	7	
Cradle	7	
Tommy	7	
Jordan	7	
Claw	6	
Jacko left hand low	6	
Alex Noren	6	
Webb	5	
The Bernhard	5	
Long	5	
Miguel claw	5	
Kooch	4	
Bryson	4	**Low Feel**
Belly	4	

Method	Safety	
Claw	9	**Low Yip potential**
Webb	9	
Kooch	9	
Bryson	9	
Belly	8	
Pencil	8	
The Bernhard	8	
Jacko left hand low	7	
Alex Noren	7	**Medium Yip potential**
Long	6	
Cradle	5	
Miguel claw	5	
Tommy	4	
Left hand low	3	
Split	3	
Jordan	3	**High Yip potential**
Jack	2	
Reverse Overlap	1	

RANKING BY FEEL

This table is dominated by the classic ways of putting used by all the greats. It's pretty obvious:

If you are a nerveless putter, then use the grip with the best feel.

RANKING BY SAFETY

The table on the right, however, is dominated by grips which limit the amount of wrist movement, and hence limit the Yip Potential. The green ones are the best if you care only about defeating the yips.

But we want to be the best we can. We want the best of *both* worlds.

THE FEEL/SAFETY COMPROMISE

When there are two factors affecting something, it is sometimes quite tricky to work out what to do. In life we are always making trade-offs between things; buy a car or a house and you are trading off price, quality, convenience, all sorts of stuff. A scientist would take some of these variables and try to create a formula to make the right choice.

Here, we have two variables for choosing a grip : Feel and Safety

Ideally, you want a grip with both feel *and* safety.

I have already mentioned that, for me, the Reverse Overlap grip has great feel but doesn't feel very *safe*.

Conversely, I've also said that the Kooch feels *safe* but I struggle with feel

"WHAT WILL PHIL DO NEXT?"

We hear this on TV commentary from time to time. Phil Mickelson is one of the most talented, mercurial golfers in history, frequently pulling off astonishing shots that other professionals would not even dare attempt. He is not afraid to experiment or innovate. Phil is the only man ever to have won a Major (the 2006 Masters) with 2 drivers in the bag. It would not surprise me to see him one day with 2 *putters* in the bag. In a way, he does already. Phil uses the reverse overlap grip for long putting – where *feel* is essential – and switches to his variation of the Claw for short putts – where *safety* is essential. It's almost like he was looking at the last 2 tables in this book.

You could try copying Phil and switch grips depending on the length of putt, but I would not recommend it. Phil is not a nervous golfer. You can't win that many tournaments if you are. He can rely happily on either stroke, switching seamlessly between them. For mortal golfers like you and me, having a choice between 2 grips for every putt will create doubt in your mind, and that is the last thing you ever need on the greens. We need to find a compromise.

COMBINED GRIP RANKING SYSTEM

Let's assume feel and safety are *equally* important in putting (which in my case they are). I will take my individual scores above for each quality and *add them up*, giving a maximum of 20. Maybe the one with the highest total is the grip I should use:

Method	Safety	Feel	Total
Maximum	10	10	20
Claw	9	6	15
Pencil	8	7	15
Webb	9	5	14
Jacko left hand low	7	6	13
Alex Noren	7	6	13
Kooch	9	4	13
Bryson	9	4	13
The Bernhard	8	5	13
Belly	8	4	12
Cradle	5	7	12
Reverse Overlap	1	10	11
Left hand low	3	8	11
Tommy	4	7	11
Jack	2	9	11
Long	6	5	11
Split	3	7	10
Miguel claw	5	5	10
Jordan	3	7	10

THIS IS THE EUREKA MOMENT

This is why I use the Claw (occasionally the Pencil). **Grip change is the biggest component of my 4 strokes per round improvement in putting.** I might try the Webb properly at some point, and I won't be impersonating Jordan Spieth again.

> **Pseudo-Science Alert:** This is based on *my* subjective view, not yours. For *you*, this table will look completely different. **Do it yourself** and see what comes out on top. It may surprise you. Go to www.scaryputter.com and download the spreadsheet.

Science Corner: Correlation between Feel and Safety in Putting

We sometimes use the word correlation to signify things are connected. Correlation is also a mathematical term.

In putting, as we have seen, it seems that *feel* and *safety* can work in opposite directions. It's difficult to have both. A scientist would describe the relationship between them as the "correlation". It is expressed as a number between -1 and +1.

If things are perfectly correlated (they act in the same way) then the correlation is +1
If they are completely unrelated (like cows and bananas) then the correlation is 0
If they are inversely correlated (they act in opposite directions) then the correlation is -1

I had a look at the correlation of my rankings of feel and safety and the answer is -0.83

So, feel and safety are *negatively* correlated for me, confirming my intuition.

This means that I have to live with the fact that feel and safety are always fighting each other in my putting.

Pseudo-Science Alert: That's as far as I will take it. We have a pragmatic, engineer's answer to what grip to try. The more mathematically-minded amongst you could take my data, plot an XY graph, create a line of best fit, and come up with an optimisation to determine the greatest outlier and therefore the optimal grip for me. That would be a waste of time. No mathematical model, no matter how smart, can get a reliable, precise answer from a set of vague inputs. If only the credit derivative market had realised that in 2007 we might never have had the Financial Crash.

DON'T BE AFRAID TO EXPERIMENT

As you may have noticed by now, I experiment a fair bit. Almost certainly too much. Padraig Harrington is a bit "laissez-faire" in comparison.

The best putters in the world tend to stick to one putter and one technique. Look at Tiger, Ben Crenshaw, the incomparable Seve, Steve Stricker. I'm so jealous. That is clearly the ideal way to play the game, but we are not starting with a blank sheet of paper here. Dealing with and preventing the yips needs something extreme. If that means changing grip, putter, everything, then that is what you need to do. Once you have found the right solution, then you can stick with that winning formula for as long as you like.

Experimenting is the only way to find what works for you, and by that I mean more than experimenting in your living room. With a bit of practice, I can hole any putt with any grip using any putter in my living room. That's not enough. You and I need the combination to work on the course, and ultimately in competition and under pressure. Take it in stages, adding more pressure to yourself each time. You will soon find out what stands up best. Be realistic; you cannot expect perfection day one.

DON'T EXPERIMENT ON THE COURSE

Experimentation isn't always good. Never do it when you are playing a serious round of golf. It's a bit like trying to the draw the ball when your body is telling you it wants to hit a fade that day. Use what you've brought to the course. Experiment again afterwards.

CONFIDENCE

Let's assume you've gone through the process of choosing a grip. You've chosen one that has a high combined ranking of feel and safety. You know that scientifically it gives you the best chance to succeed. This all helps to build your confidence, and that very confidence will help prevent any yips from surfacing.

In addition, if you have a second safe grip available, that knowledge will perversely reduce the likelihood of ever having to use it.

You've made the most important step of the journey and you're on the way.

CHAPTER

11

WHAT PUTTER SHOULD YOU USE?

When the putting demons have taken hold, it is quite understandable to clutch at any straw available. The most obvious one is your useless putter. When you are sick and tired of watching it misbehave, it seems reasonable, even necessary, to change it.

A NEW PUTTER IS NOT A BIG ENOUGH CHANGE.
At the height of my putting woes during the "Lost Decades", I once purchased a putter *during* my round of golf. I was on holiday on the Isle of Wight, playing on my own with a half set of clubs. Pretty much the lowest stress form of golf available. My putting was so bad on the front nine that when I re-encountered the pro shop next to the 10th tee, I selected a brand-new putter and bought it. From memory, I think it was an Odyssey 2-ball. It behaved for 2 holes, beyond which it was slightly worse than its predecessor. I no longer have it. You would think I learnt a lesson that day, but – like second marriages – buying a new putter is a triumph of optimism over experience. I've bought plenty since and have an embarrassingly large number in my "stable". Very few are on the playing rota.

Randomly switching your putter to one that looks nice, or a bit different, or even one whose sole merit is that it isn't the one you were previously using, is unlikely to be a long-term solution.

Swapping putter can be like changing a hubcap on a car whose engine has blown. You're still going nowhere.

Constantly changing putters is a *symptom* of the problem, not the solution.

A different putter can create light relief, but nothing more than that unless it is radically different.

However, there can be *good* reasons to change putter, but let's stick to the logic of our definition of the yips and see if we can unearth any clues as to what putter might help us.

"an inability to control the putter at impact due to involuntary muscle spasms".

Our intention is to eliminate those involuntary muscle spasms using a new technique and a refreshed mental attitude, thereby allowing you to use pretty much whatever putter you fancy.

However, the mental game is about confidence, and if you believe your putter will prevent or minimise the effects of the yips then that can only be a good thing.

HIGH MOI PUTTERS
For instance, a putter with a high Moment of Inertia (MOI) will generally twist less and rotate less. The physics behind this is rock solid. The weight of the putter is spread out as far as possible from its centre of mass so that it literally takes more force to twist it. It stands to reason therefore that a yipped putt using a high MOI putter will be less bad than one using a blade. It still won't be pretty though, but it's a step in the right direction.

HEAVY/COUNTERBALANCED PUTTERS
Similarly, counterbalanced putters (with extra weight in both the head and the grip) are a good way of increasing total inertia and minimising the effects of a twitch whilst maintaining a reasonable swing weight. My road to recovery began with the imaginatively named "Heavy Putter", which certainly lived up to the billing but was eventually discarded as it really is too heavy either to carry or to have any idea with distance putting.

Anyone struggling with a twitchy putter should consider trying something a little heavier, perhaps counterbalanced. Blades are best left to the kids and tour pros.

TOE-HANG OR FACE-BALANCED?
The other key variable with putters is the "toe-hang". I never used to understand what this meant, even though I pretended I did. Essentially, all it means is whether the line of the shaft goes through the centre of mass of the putter head or not. You can test this by balancing your putter on your finger somewhere near the middle of the shaft. You will see that with a blade putter the toe of the putter hangs down. A "face-balanced putter" will have the face horizontal and pointing up to the sky.

Toe-hang Putter

Face-balanced Putter

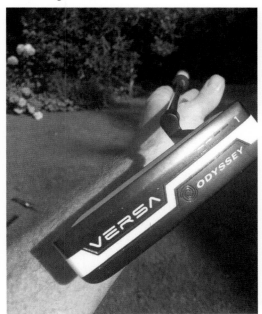 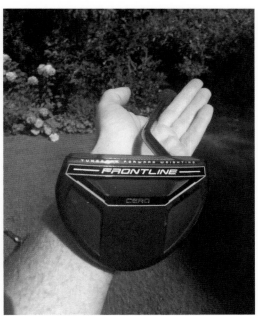

Toe-hang putters are supposedly for rotational putting strokes; face-balanced mallets more for "back and through" strokes. If you are suffering with your putting, I would suggest you probably don't need more rotation, so my preference is for a face-balanced mallet of some type.

Clearly, there is a compromise to be struck.

The Feel/Function trade-off with putters is like the Feel/Safety trade-off with your grip.

Be aware of what trade-off you are making and try to make a rational decision.

Big, heavy mallet putters may help on short putts, but if they fail to get the distance right on your long putts then you will still struggle. I think there is even an argument for having a heavy, high MOI putter for short putts and a lighter blade for long putts (the equipment equivalent of Phil Mickelson using 2 different grips) , but in practice that is not only a bit embarrassing (you shouldn't care about this by the way) but you will be forever questioning which one to use. On the course you need certainty, not doubt.

Add to the mix the fact that you may be trying loads of different styles of putting. Each of those may well lend itself to a different style or weight of putter. Try several putters and slowly whittle them down until you have "The One". It is not an easy process but once you settle on one, *put all the others away* so you cannot get distracted. Taking several putters to the course is not the road to success.

GRIP SIZE

There is a generally accepted agreement in golf that larger grips can "help keep the hands quiet". As someone for whom quiet hands were for many years a forlorn hope, that sounds pretty tempting. My years of experimentation have found this size theory to be unproven, although I do like some extra weight in the grip. Results for me have been reasonably uniform across the spectrum of grip sizes.

Some grip positions lend themselves to a large grip (the Cradle is one that springs to mind), whilst others do not. It is very much a matter of personal preference, but I would say that because the fingers are so rarely to blame for the yips, it is quite nice to have them involved. They are one of the most sensitive parts of the body, so a finger grip is probably going to have lots of feel. Sometimes I find it easier to get the fingers involved using a small grip.

WHAT PUTTER DO I USE?

Sadly, it is not the Scotty Cameron Newport blade I dream of. It is a very unfashionable, old, slightly heavy, counterbalanced, face-balanced, smallish mallet made by TaylorMade. A decent compromise of stability on short putts and feel on long ones. The grip is a midsize 15-inch Winn one that came as standard. I'm trying really hard to stick to it, but in the background I know I have several other putters that work reasonably well. It's a bit like knowing I could put a different grip into play if I needed to. Perversely, when you have other acceptable putters available on the bench, there is far less risk of needing to make the substitution.

The Bag of Shame: part of the collection I assembled as a Pretend Normal putter.

Science Corner: What Putter should you use?

Can we do better than "Pick the one you like, with maybe a bit of help thrown in"?

Here are some of the factors we all consider when buying a putter:

- Looks — Do you like looking down at it?
- Feel — How does it feel when you stroke it?
- Safety — How stable and yip-free is it for your stroke?
- Type — Is it short, armlock or long?
- Acclimatisation — How long will it take to get used to it?
- Price — Is it decent value?
- Availability — It's tricky to get hold of some armlock and long putters.
- Fit — Short putters are easy to fit, others aren't.
- Prestige — Do you like to be seen with a top-end putter?

That's way too many variables. Let's cut them down.

We'll assume you are comparing putters you already own, so type, acclimatisation, price, availability and fit can be deleted.

We also care about results, so prestige is out. Leave your ego at home.

We are left with 3 variables to use for our decision: **Looks, Feel and Safety**.

Here are a few of my putters and the score I give them out of 10 for each category:

Putter	Score		
	Looks	**Feel**	**Safety**
Scotty Cameron Newport	9	8	5
Bettinardi Studio	8	7	6
Taylormade spide mallet	7	7	8
Bettinardi Kuchar Armlock	7	5	8
Odyssey Rossie	7	7	7
Evnroll	7	6	6
Odyssey#1versa	6	7	6
Cleveland Frontline	6	6	6
Odyssey Long	5	5	7

I've ranked them by looks here. Who can disagree with the Scotty at the top? The ranking by *feel* is almost identical.

But how about if we are a bit nervous? We need to be pragmatic, swallow our pride and choose based on Safety first, followed by feel and then looks.

Let's give a score out of 10 for the importance of each attribute. Here are mine:

	Weighting			
	Looks	**Feel**	**Safety**	**Total**
My Rating	3	5	10	18

You can see that I value safety twice as much as feel and over 3 times as much as looks.

Now I am going to do a **Weighted Average Calculation**, giving higher relative value to the scores in the quality I find more important.

	Weighting			
	Looks	**Feel**	**Safety**	**Total**
My Rating	3	5	10	18

Putter	Score			Weighted Average
	Looks	**Feel**	**Safety**	
Taylormade spide mallet	7	7	8	7.6
Bettinardi Kuchar Armlock	7	5	8	7.0
Odyssey Rossie	7	7	7	7.0
Bettinardi Studio	8	7	6	6.6
Scotty Cameron Newport	9	8	5	6.5
Odyssey#1versa	6	7	6	6.3
Evnroll	7	6	6	6.2
Odyssey Long	5	5	7	6.1
Cleveland Frontline	6	6	6	6.0

The TaylorMade comes out on top, and sadly the Scotty is mid-table at best.

Pseudo-Science Alert: These are my numbers. Yours will be different. The range of weighted average ratings is quite small, confirming that **putter choice is difficult**. I would definitely not go further with this maths, but as a framework it confirms my gut feeling that the TaylorMade spider mallet is a good compromise for me.

This is a quite a procedure, but is useful **because it makes you declare what your priorities are**. You can do this analysis too by going to www.scaryputter.com and downloading the Excel spreadsheet.

If Mr Pretend Normal went through this process, he might swap his prestigious, expensive putter for something that gives him more chance of holing putts.

(In 1988, I used exactly this weighted average analysis to decide which car to buy. At the time, my biggest constraint was cost. Consequently, its weighting was so high that I ended up buying the cheapest car of the alternatives – an MG Metro – rather than the one I really wanted – a Volkswagen Golf GTi. It was one of the worst decisions I have ever made. No system is perfect)

12

THE MENTAL GAME

All I need to do in this chapter is convince you that you love putting, that it is the easiest and most enjoyable part of the game and that you simply can't wait to show off your prowess on the greens.

You may not realise this, but **you have already completed much of the work**, or at the very least you have read about the work required.

- You have identified your yip signature: You know what the problem is ✔
- You have chosen the best grip that will minimise your problem ✔
- You have selected the best putter to make it work ✔

Just knowing this should give you confidence, and as we all know, confidence is essential for good putting.

These steps will also have resolved your neurological issues, so here is how the graph in Chapter 6 should now look:

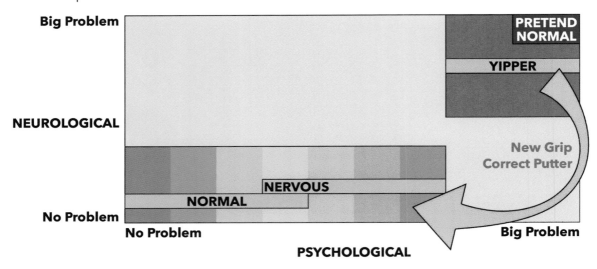

GOLF PSYCHOLOGY

Bob Rotella is the world's leading expert on golf psychology. I know my place, and it is not at his side. He has coached many Major champions. He has written many excellent books about golf, some specifically about putting. Read them. I particularly recommend "Golf is not a game of Perfect", "Putting out of your Mind", "The Unstoppable Golfer" and "Your 15th Club". That should be enough for now. It is impossible to summarise his teachings, but I think he would agree if I said he wants you to develop a reliable, consistent process for putting and not worry about the outcome.

The following are some of my thoughts on the game, heavily influenced by Dr Bob.

THE GOLFER'S MIND

Let's first of all make a comparison between a tour pro and a yipper to see what mental differences we can unearth:

Attribute	Tour Pro	Yipper
Putting Routine	Consistent	Inconsistent
Time taken	Consistent	Random
Mental Approach	Positive	Negative
Objective	Hole it	Don't 3-putt
Thoughts	Target	I hope I don't yip this I don't fancy this one I don't like putting Shall I try a different stroke? Shall I have another look at the hole? Shall I take it straight back or on the inside? What part of the ball should I look at? I missed one like this on the last hole Which "big muscle" should I be using? I hope I get this close enough to tap in the next What will my partners think if I miss this? Shall I start my backswing yet?
Reaction to Holing	Acceptance	Relief, Surprise, Joy
Reaction to Missing	Acceptance	Anger, Denial, Grief, Despair, Shame

DEVELOP A CONSISTENT ROUTINE

Remember the Rhythm Method I described in the chapter about different ways of approaching putting problems? I gave it a score of 9/10. It's probably even more important than that.

I don't really care what the routine is. Watch the best guys in the world. They all do it differently:

Some take up to 5 practice strokes with the putter; others take none.
Some step straight to the ball; others prefer to start behind it facing the hole.
Some line up the ball then step away again.
Some look at the target 5 times, some only once.
Some have a forward press to trigger the putt.
Some lift the putter to initiate the stroke.

There is huge variety, but they all have three things in common:

- They all choose their target and commit to it.
- They all follow exactly the same sequence on every putt.
- It always takes the same amount of time.

Professionals are equally consistent with the long game. Every tour pro knows that when the pressure is on, he needs to stick to his routine. Any variation or delay allows doubt to creep in, allows the brain to start thinking, to make decisions, to try new things. These are all undesirable.

When it's crunch time in a tournament and you see a player put in an extra practice stroke, you know he is in trouble.

DEVELOPING A ROUTINE IS DIFFICULT

I find it extremely hard. **Ken Brown** says in his book "One Putt" that it took him **4 weeks** to develop his when he was working with Henry Cotton in the Algarve. That is incredible.

Choose a sequence that is not overly long but has a flow to it. A stationary golfer is one prone to thinking too much. You do not want to be a statue.

Then you need to go to the putting green and repeat that sequence, ideally hundreds of times until it has found its way into your subconscious and becomes automatic.

Go back and do it the next day, and the next. It is a real commitment, but the payoff is huge.

I am not good at this, particularly in relation to the number of practice strokes I take. One of the few times I did it well was in regional qualifying for the Open at Burhill in 2017. I diligently practiced my putting routine for the week beforehand. On the actual day, I had to face 4-footers on each of the last 3 greens. For me, with my history, that is huge pressure. I managed to stick to the routine and luckily, they went in. Without a routine to rely on I think I would have failed.

I can think of a few incidents more recently where I have let the routine slip and the results have been much more disappointing. I need to work on it.

BE A CAVEMAN

You may not have realised this, but you are a living miracle. Think back in time and consider how many hundreds of generations of ancestors you have had. An unbroken line of forebears, all of whom managed to escape being eaten, killed or maimed before passing their genes on to their offspring. The chances of you existing at all are infinitesimally small, and yet you exist. Whilst nowadays we all have very specialised pastimes, the vast majority of our ancestors were hunters, with a few hunter/gatherers or farmers thrown in. The genes you have inherited are those of successful fighters and survivors, none of whom ever wondered too deeply about their spear-throwing technique. The ability to aim at a target and allow your instincts to take over is within us all. You certainly have the innate ability to roll a ball towards a hole. Don't overcomplicate things. Just trust thousands of years of evolution and let it happen.

EMPTY YOUR MIND

For some reason, golfers tend to be very inward-looking, prone to over-analysis, over-complication, over-experimentation and a fair bit of self-criticism. Whilst that is essential in some walks of life, when it comes to hitting a putt on a golf course, it is useless. Contrary to what you might do at home while you are experimenting, on the course everything needs to be as simple as possible. A yipper's mind is very busy; full of thoughts, worries, feelings, scar tissue, mostly bad, mostly unhelpful. You don't need any of them.

The *only* things you need to feel on the course are;
- You're focussed on your target, trying to hole the putt
- It doesn't matter if you don't hole it

Let's take these points separately:

TRY TO HOLE THE PUTT

It seems obvious that you should be trying to hole the putt, but sometimes that can get lost in the mental mist. Most yippers completely lose sight of this simple goal, usually replacing it with some kind of negative thought.

FALSE EXPECTATIONS

One of the reasons golfers develop the yips is that they have false impressions of how successful pro golfers are at putting. Watch a tournament on TV and the coverage will provide a biased impression of putting:

- These are the best putters in the world.
- The coverage is of the leaders, who by definition are having a good putting week.
- The TV producers choose to show footage of golfers holing putts rather than missing them.

The combination of these factors makes it seem like a 7-foot putt is trivial and you must be useless if you don't hole one. Each year, only the top 30 in the world will hole more than 60% of putts between 5 and 10 feet. The average PGA Tour pro barely holes half of them and the worst on tour are around 45%. It's completely normal to miss these putts, even for the best in the game, so there is no need to beat yourself up if you miss one.

DON'T WORRY ABOUT OUTCOMES

Loads of good putts miss. There are too many variables, even *after* you have made contact. It could miss for reasons entirely out of your control. Greens are not perfect. Your read could have been a little out. Making everything depend on the outcome only serves to pile the pressure on yourself. Be happy if you feel you have made a decent stroke. In the words of Rudyard Kipling at the start of the book:

"If you can meet with Triumph and Disaster. And treat those two imposters just the same..."

MINIMISE IMPACT

Think back to the section about identifying your yip signature. If you did the same exercise, practicing your stroke separately with each hand, but doing so without a ball, what do you think would happen? It might surprise you to learn that in many cases the player's yip disappears when the ball is not there. The uncontrolled flinch only occurs when there is an impact. Clearly, we can't take the ball away on the golf course, but as far as possible it is better to imagine it is not there. Sticking to your routine is the best way to achieve this, because it subordinates impact to just one tiny part of an automatic, subconscious movement. However, here are a few more things that may help distract your mind. Some of them we have come across before:

- Close your eyes (Sergio Garcia)
- Look at the hole (Jordan Spieth)
- Look at a spot 6 inches in front of the ball, over which you want the ball to roll. I particularly like this alternative as you can look at your target whilst still keeping the ball and clubhead in your field of vision.
- Imagine (but don't look at) the entire path your putter is taking, including follow-through.
- Focus mentally on where you want the putter to be (and where it should be facing) at the end of the stroke.

Most of these techniques involve focussing on a point or an event after impact, thereby taking attention away from the impact itself. I think all of them are useful whilst practising. Major champions use these techniques on the course too. For me, I prefer to use what I call the Quiet Eye, even if I have perhaps got the name wrong.

QUIET EYE

There is some talk in golf coaching circles about "Quiet eye" and what it means. Generally, the research suggest that expert putters remain focused on the ball for a longer period of time than amateurs. Approximately twice as long, and importantly they remain looking at where the ball used to be after impact. Some people find it useful to have a dot on the ball to help retain this focus.

For me, quiet eye means something quite different. I agree that you do not want your eyes darting around, but I much prefer a soft focus on the ball. While I am putting, I try to imagine a picture of my target in my head. My eyes aren't closed, but I'm not really focused on the ball at all. Focus on the ball can lead to focus on impact and we really want to get away from that. Just think target.

DON'T WORRY ABOUT OTHER PEOPLE

When you have the yips, you know that everybody is watching you. It makes things doubly difficult wondering what they might think if you miss your 3-footer. When you rock up with your new counterbalanced putter and sporting your new claw grip, they will know something's up. What will they think of you?

Ignore them. You don't care.

In general, I am an advocate for taking notice of what your playing partners are doing; keep quiet when they are playing, don't step on their lines on the green, be ready to play when it's your turn.

However, this does not extend to worrying about what they think of your game. Your playing partners are probably too obsessed with their own games to pay much attention to yours. When you address the ball, your partners should not exist. Your focus should be solely on your target.

SELECTIVE MEMORY

Bob Rotella has a routine he recommends. You lie in bed at night and think about your last round of golf. Easy, but you only think about the *good* shots you hit, and keep replaying them in your mind. Eventually, you create hard-wired memories of great shots and fool yourself that you're a better golfer than you really are. It sounds ridiculous but it works. It helped Padraig Harrington win the Open.

There is a corollary to this. The one thing you mustn't do is replay the bad shots in your head. This applies equally when you are still on the course.

I have become quite good at this, to such an extent that if I don't write down my score, I sometimes find it hard to remember at the end of the round what I did on each hole. If I am playing match play, I struggle to know what the score is. It can be embarrassing.

DON'T GET ANGRY

It isn't easy, but whatever happens on the course, leave it behind. The next shot is the only one that matters. The last one is not only irrelevant, but you should behave as if it never happened. There are some sports which require anger and aggression. Golf is not one of them. The angry, chuntering golfer makes poor decisions, may alienate his playing partners, and will take more shots. He may also become the butt of his friends' jokes.

Tiger famously only allowed himself to be angry about a shot within a 6 foot radius of where he hit it, but once he stepped out of that circle he forgot about it (of course if you've only hit your drive 6 inches this technique isn't going to work very well). Tyrrell Hatton appears to be particularly adept at this. He is quick to complain after a poor shot, but seems to have a highly effective reset button.

This approach is particularly useful and necessary for putting. If you miss a putt, you are going to be hitting your next shot very soon, and you have little time to re-establish your inner calm. Focus only on the next shot.

PRETEND YOU ARE SOMEONE ELSE

Seriously? First, you suggest brainwashing yourself at night and now this? Yes, seriously.

Have you watched teenagers putt? Carefree, fearless, perhaps a little rash. No kid would consider anything but trying to hole a putt. It is the complete opposite end of the spectrum to a yipper. Pretend you are a kid, or if that seems too difficult or generic, here's another idea. Be more specific; think about tour pros.

WATCH PRO GOLF IN DETAIL

I like watching golf on television. Perhaps I watch too much. Members of my family frequently ask me in bewilderment what it is I find interesting. Fair question. With the exception of the Majors and the Ryder Cup, I accept that there isn't a great deal of drama. What I do is watch the swing, the technique, the head movement, the grip, the shoulder turn, the leg movement, the body language. For every shot, I play a game in which I guess where the ball went versus where the player was intending to hit it. It's a little sad, I admit. I never claimed to be great company at dinner parties.

However, one of the benefits (perhaps the only one) is that I am now extremely familiar with many tour pros' golf swings. When I am playing, I occasionally have a bizarre, out of body experience where a pro golfer's name unexpectedly pops into my head during my swing. Presumably, this is because what I am doing feels like what I recall seeing on the telly. Sadly, I don't get a Rory McIlroy vibe very often. Yes, Jim Furyk has turned up but only when I took the club back massively on the outside. Perhaps the weirdest one was Geoff Ogilvy, who I hadn't watched for years and just came out of nowhere.

IMPERSONATE A PRO

Let's get back to the point. Rather than waiting to see who turns up, you can be proactive and take control for yourself. Choose a golfer whose putting stroke you admire and impersonate them. This can really work well, but you must also be realistic. I know what happens if I imitate Seve's beautiful putting stroke. It doesn't end well. But the lightness of his grip is worth copying. Rickie Fowler picks the club off the ground just before taking it away. Pretty handy if you are getting stuck at address. I love Brandt Snedeker's perpetual motion pre-shot routine. I love Alex Noren's forward press. I am currently impersonating Webb Simpson's right-hand grip and brisk tempo on the greens, even though I don't like the look of the rest of his game.

You don't need to copy the whole stroke, maybe just one element or just the pre-shot routine. Copy someone else and there is less room in your head for any of your own nonsense.

POSITIVE PUTTING

Golfers who suffer from the yips (and many who don't) can soon become very tentative on the greens, trying to lag the ball near the hole so they do not have one of those nasty 3 to 6 footers on the way back. I fully understand the feeling, but this approach often leaves the putt that same distance short, and most importantly removes any possibility of holing the *first* putt. In addition, tentative putting can often have a deceleration in the stroke, and that is just the worst thing possible.

Here are a few games you can play to help you with this; the first is for practice and the others for when you are on the course and the pressure is greater.

Practice Putting Game

Let's assume your practice putting green has 9 holes, all of them a reasonable distance apart (maybe 15 to 30 feet). Play a putting round with one ball, holing out at each hole and adding up the score. Simple so far, eh?

The only difference is that for every putt you leave short you must add a shot. As an example, if you leave a 15-footer 1 inch short then you count 3 for the hole (assuming you managed to snake in that tricky 1-incher). Count your total score at the end of the first lap. It will probably be high, shockingly high perhaps, much higher than the 18 strokes you might reasonably expect to take without the penalty shots. Don't worry. This is just a game, and it gives you loads of room for improvement. Improvement is a great reinforcer of learning.

Keep doing laps and trying to beat your score. Quite quickly the penny will drop that leaving a putt short has such a high penalty that you might as well be much more aggressive. You will over-hit some putts, but slowly you will acclimatise to hitting the ball past the hole. It is an obvious truism, but hitting the ball at least as far as the hole is essential to hole a putt.

Play this game as much as you can, and you will be well on the way to reversing the tentativeness that pervades the yipper's mind.

On Course Game #1

Every time you play, set yourself a target for the total length of putts you hole during the round. Let's say 72 feet, which is an average of 4 feet per hole (the second piece of rigorous maths in the book. My university tutor would be so proud).

This can completely transform the way you think about putting. Suddenly, every putt becomes an opportunity to get closer to that goal. Stand over a 40-footer on the first. Hole it and you are over halfway to your target. How good would that be? Playing this game and thinking this way really encourages you to be positive. You may not attain your 72 feet target, but that doesn't matter. Trying to reach it will make you a better, much more positive putter.

The *best* putting stat for the PGA tour is Total Strokes Gained.
The *second* best is this game; Total Feet Holed

Total Feet Holed is a much more volatile statistic and less reliable, but it is still very good. There is an extremely high correlation between the ranking of the players on both lists.

The top guys on tour average around 80 feet per round, a little over 4 feet per hole.

Why then would I suggest setting a target of 72 feet for you, which is better than many guys on the PGA tour?

On their good days, tour pros average way more than that. This game is about being positive, trying to have a good day, trying to hole even the long putts, and continuing to do so until the end of your round. Even if you're having a bad day, you may still hit your target if you hole a 40-footer on the last green. Set too low a target and there is a risk you will become complacent.

For tour pros, the target number would always be over 100 feet and probably closer to 150 feet.

On Course Game #2

Game #1 is about outcomes but is really an encouragement to be positive. Game #2 is about process and letting go. Instead of counting your putts or the distances you holed, instead give each putt a rating. The rating should be based purely on your process

Did you follow your routine?
Did you focus on your target?
Did you try and hole the putt?
Did you make a decent stroke?

Give yourself a score out of 10. If you did all the above well but you didn't hole it, it doesn't matter. Give yourself a 10. We are completely taking the outcome out of the equation. Equally, if you managed to hole a putt without really committing to it, mark yourself down. Be honest.

Just try and maximise your average score. This game is highly effective and can eventually help remove the fear of missing that is the destructive heart of the yips.

13

PUTTING IT ALL TOGETHER

You've made it. Now you know how to fix the yips, but let's just confirm it shall we?

Remember in Chapter 6 when we said that in order to fix the yips you need to solve both the *neurological* problem and the *psychological* one? Let's have a look at what we have done and whether we have achieved both goals.

Fix	Neurological Benefit	Psychological Benefit
Identify your Yip Signature	✔	✘
Change to an optimal grip	✔	✔
Choose a putter that helps	✔	✔
Develop a consistent, flowing routine	✘	✔
Putt like you don't care	✘	✔
Result	✔	✔

That's all there is to it. If all has gone to plan, then you are ready to sing along with the Righteous Brothers: "You've Lost That Yipping Feeling".

Here's how our graph now looks:

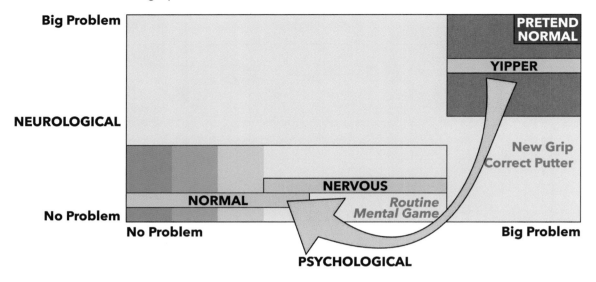

IT'S A WAR NOT A BATTLE

Let me offer a note of caution at this point. This is not an instant fix. It will take time. Probably a few months. It took me longer than that, but I developed the yips in a different age, when information and advice about them didn't' really exist. Maybe I was also a slow learner. It is also important to recognise (in the same way perhaps that an alcoholic does) that you will always feel some kind of weakness, even if it is just the scar tissue in your head.

ATTACK ON ALL FRONTS

Dealing with the yips needs to be a little like how we treat AIDS. Thirty years ago, it was a death sentence. Today, there is still no actual cure for AIDS, but a combination of retroviral drugs can pretty much keep it at bay indefinitely, and have turned it into a manageable chronic disorder within a normal life.

None of those retroviral drugs will work on its own. The AIDS virus is an elusive beast, constantly mutating and rendering any one individual treatment ineffective. But if you use 3 or more treatments then the combined effect of the drugs is to suppress and control the virus.

Your task with putting demons is to combine all the elements you have learnt in a similar fashion. Don't rely just on a new putter or a new grip or a breathing routine. Use belt and braces and perhaps an extra pair of underpants just in case. You need the combined power to keep the beast at bay. Even Harry Potter didn't defeat Voldemort completely on his own.

REPEAT AND REINFORCE

During Covid lockdown, I wasn't allowed to play golf, but I was able to practice my chipping in the back garden. I was making really poor contact (no, not the yips – nothing to see here) and decided to look for help in my golf library. I opened up a book which at first read had done nothing for me and had another look. To my surprise, it seemed way better second time around. In fact, I would go so far as to say it's the only book you need on the subject. If you are wondering, it is "Your Short Game Solution" by James Sieckmann. Quite how I didn't notice that initially I do not know, but it made me realise that **skim-reading an instruction book doesn't work**. You need to re-read it and highlight the important bits. Anyone serious about improving needs the occasional reminder.

(It is much easier to review and revise from a physical book. If you have been reading this book as an e-book and think you may wish to refer to it again, consider buying the paperback version.)

A QUICK FIX

What? You have just told me it's a war not a battle, and now you're telling me that just like some cheap whodunnit I could have skipped all the pre-amble and found out the answer on the back page?

Not quite. There really are no short cuts, but after long consideration I am prepared to get off my high horse and offer you my best quick-fix recommendation:

- Use the Claw with your dominant hand.
- Use a counterbalanced, face balanced mallet.
- Use no more than a 10-second routine from start to finish.
- Never let the putter head stop moving for more than 1 second.
- Impersonate Brandt Snedeker.
- Putt like you don't care.

The problem with this is that it almost certainly will not suit you perfectly, if at all, and it may raise your expectations unreasonably high. You have been warned.

ENJOYING GOLF AGAIN

Let's go back to where we began and consider Bernhard. How many times has he changed his putting style? Plenty. Is this because the bad thoughts kept creeping back in? Perhaps, but he has found a way to keep them at bay for decades whilst playing golf at the highest level under the greatest of pressure. Like him (and me), you can find a way to operate without them appearing, even if you never completely forget that the yips once existed. Maybe Bernhard *can* forget. I wonder if cyborgs can delete memories from their hard drives.

It is OK for golfers to feel stress, to look up too soon, to miss short putts, to come out of shots. Being nervous is part of the game and needs to be embraced. Even when you have successfully gone through all the steps discussed in this book, you will still feel all these things. You will still have bad days. You will hit some dodgy putts. But you can be confident that you are on the right track. Stay on it, and one day you will realise you have stopped yipping.

Then you can get on with your life and finally read all the other putting books. They will help you master posture, alignment, green reading, distance judgement, eye dominance and the all-important question of "which putt breaks more, an uphill one or a downhill one?"

14

ACKNOWLEDGEMENTS & LESSONS LEARNED

Sorry, but I am going to break with convention and make the acknowledgements an entire chapter. Breaking with convention doesn't trouble me too much. I'm the man who put the Drake equation in a golf book. I fear it may be even worse than one of those endless Oscars acceptance speeches.

Having run out of things to say about putting, I was rather surprised to discover that I still had a couple of thoughts to get out there. This may be the only book I ever write, and it may be the only chance to give thanks where it is due. This chapter will be the closest I can get to sincerity, and the furthest away from humour. That may be a matter of great relief and small recompense for you.

Many thanks to my beautiful wife for 25 years of happy marriage and her tolerance of my many shortcomings. I love you. The same to my 3 children whom I love dearly and equally. Recently they have all even started to take an interest in golf. I couldn't be more happy or proud.

Thanks and apologies to Bernhard Langer. You showed us it was possible. Even though I have been very rude about you, I trust you understand that I would never wish to offend one of my heroes. I respect you immensely, and I suspect that we may actually be quite alike. I have Germanic genes too.

Thanks to Jack, Tom and Seve for their inspiration. They say you should never meet your heroes and I've done a decent job of sticking to that principle. Tom Watson is the only one I met, and he dealt with this starstruck, incoherent idiot with great charm and dignity, particularly as he was about to tee off in a senior Major. He is a true gentleman of the game.

The experience of writing this book has been a real eye-opener for me. My respect for all writers has risen immensely. I have found it incredibly challenging, but great fun and utterly obsessive. It has compelled me to get out of bed several times in the middle of the night to get my thoughts down before amnesia kicked in. I've had less sleep than when the children were young, even taking into account the fact that I never did the lion's share of night duty. I now understand a small amount of the hard work and dedication that went into my favourite golf books, written by (alphabetically so there is no fighting):

Mark Broadie, Ken Brown, Tom Cox, Tom Coyne, Lawrence Donegan, John Feinstein, Hank Haney, John Jacobs, Henry Longhurst, Phil Mickelson, Karl Morris, Jack Nicklaus, Gary Nicol, Dave Pelz, Harvey Penick, Rick Reilly, Bob Rotella, James Sieckmann, Dave Stockton, Stan Utley and PG Wodehouse. Thank you everybody.

Thanks to the many friends I have played golf with over the years. In particular, I would like to mention the members of the MWMs, whose characters I have been systematically assassinating throughout this book. The MWMs play 4 ball matches regularly in the South East of England and elsewhere, arranged enthusiastically by our intense Honorary Secretary. The most distinguishing feature of the society is that the result of each game requires a match report. At our annual dinner there is a hotly contested Scribe's award for that year's finest piece of penmanship (my next bestseller will be a compilation of the top 100). The outstanding all-time winner was the succinct "It rained. We lost", but with so many matches going on, and so much at stake, there has been a tendency to stray far from the topic of golf in order to find an innovative new hook on which to hang the results of a golf match. My misjudged attempt to adapt Lewis Carroll's poem Jabberwocky was perhaps the worst example of this. Every time I play golf with these friends, I am reminded what joy and friendship I would have denied myself had I succumbed to the yips and given up golf. This book is my entry for the 2020 Scribe's award.

Thanks to my golf teachers; Hugh Marr (who showed me how to get out of bunkers), Jon Woodroffe (who is the second most positive person I have ever met) and Ian Clark (who keeps telling me I have a rubbish backswing).

Thanks to Richard Pennell and the heathland gem that is Woking Golf Club for allowing me to be a member there for 30 years and for acting both on the cover and as backdrop for my son's excellent photographs in this book.

Thanks to all the scientists out there. The first draft of this book had a large number of references to "geeks" and "nerds". I'm perfectly happy to refer to myself that way, but scientists deserve more respect than that. They are rarely the loudest voice in the room and consequently rarely get the thanks they deserve. Take a look at your mobile phone and ask yourself if an arts graduate could have produced it. We live in a world where opinion increasingly seems to matter more than facts or logic. During the last 6 months I have watched many politicians and scientists standing next to each other talking about coronavirus. The strongest conclusion I have drawn is that we need more scientists and fewer politicians. Maybe government should just contain more scientists and engineers and fewer Politics, Philosophy and Economics graduates. I don't think it is a coincidence that Angela Merkel is a physicist and Germany has handled the crisis better than most. Whilst I have spent the last 30 years working in a bank and fiddling around with golf clubs, a friend of mine has been one of those scientists I mentioned working on a cure for AIDS. I know who has contributed more to society.

Another friend of mine is involved with the R&A, and recently informed me that if I make any money from this book it will breach the rules of amateur status and I would have to turn pro (even if I am likely to make more money coming third in a monthly medal at Woking). I've already had a dabble with the pro ranks and I don't think they would be quaking in their boots if I turned up on the first tee in my scruffy chinos and lucky jumper. Luckily, there is another solution. The proceeds from this book will go to Great Ormond Street Hospital Children's Charity, thereby allowing you and me to contribute in our own small way to society.

Thank you to the many people who helped and advised on this book: Alan Hodson, Simon Bunce, Roger Bathurst, Richard Palmer, Richard Pennell, Christian Marquardt, Hugh Marr, Mark Watson, Carl Bianco, Ian Clark and many others. The first draft of the book had way more jokes. Some of these kind people gently let me know that they weren't very funny. Most of the jokes have gone. Look at the ones that remain and imagine how bad the others must have been. It took me a while to realise that if people were reading the book it was primarily to improve their putting, not to indulge my desire to show I'm clever. Writing a book is very enlightening. I recommend it.

I'm a newcomer when it comes to prose, but I can confidently state that the hardest part of writing a book is choosing the title. Here are a few I (and others) came up with and rejected: Yips Apocalypse; Eclipse the Yips; Yipping Point; The Putting Paradox; Shame and Glory : My Yips Story; Yesterday's Yips; The Yips : Return to Sender; Sgt. Jacko's Lonely Yip Club Band; From Yips to Eternity; The Yips Initiative; The Yips Hypothesis; Goodbye Mr. Yips; Read My Lips, No More Yips; Gimme Gimme Gimme No Yips After Midnight; Yips Don't Lie; Yips Survival Guide; Proven Tips to Cure the Yips; Confessions of a Former Yipper; Unzip the Yips; Beat the Yips, not Yourself; You've Lost That Yipping Feeling; Nightmare on Yip Street; Yip Zero to Golf Hero; Scary Putter and the Curse of the Yips; Scary Putter and the Ice-cool Prince; Scary Putter and the Cyborg Phoenix; Scary Putter and the Chamber of Horrors; Yip Yip Away; Yipfulness; Putting Poison; The Putting Predicament; Trouble with Putting; and my personal favourite, How Not to be Such a Totally Shit Putter.

Scary Putter survived in the name of my website www.scaryputter.com If you need any advice choosing a title for your own book, you can contact me there.

My final and undying thanks go to my real heroes, who of course are my parents and to whom I owe the most.

My father introduced me to the game and loved it as much as I do. He was a late convert to golf, only taking to it in his 40s but quickly getting down to a single figure handicap. He played for the Lytham Seniors team and once excitedly told me that he had just beaten someone who had played in The Open. I still have his hole-in-one balls on my bookshelf, next to Golf My Way. When I was 14, he and I travelled in great anticipation to Scotland where we both played our first ever rounds on the Old Course at St Andrews. I was astonished to discover such a magical town, where it was not embarrassing to confess that you were a golfer. Everywhere you looked was golf, whether the hallowed turf of The Old Course itself, or the people carrying their pencil bags in the street, or the shops selling strange old wooden putters. I was in heaven. So was he. Sadly, 6 weeks later he was suddenly taken ill and died. 14 is not a good age to lose your parent and hero. I would love to have had more time to know him as a friend as well as a father, but it made me very proud this year, 40 years after our trip to St Andrews, to be invited to become a member of the Royal & Ancient Golf Club. I hope he would have been proud too.

My mother, the source of my German genes, was the rock of our family. Hers was a life of many interests (none of them golf), which she pursued to the highest level whilst managing our family singlehandedly. She passed away 30 years to the day after my Dad.

Thank you both for everything.

Printed in Great Britain
by Amazon